12/03

A TRAVEL GUIDE TO

Medieval
Constantinople

Other books in the Travel Guide series:

A TRAVEL GUIDE TO

Medieval
Constantinople

James Barter

LUCENT
BOOKS ®

THOMSON

GALE

San Diego • Detroit • New York • San Francisco • Cleveland • New Haven, Conn. • Waterville, Maine • London • Munich

© 2003 by Lucent Books. Lucent Books is an imprint of The Gale Group, Inc.,
a division of Thomson Learning, Inc.

Lucent Books® and Thomson Learning™ are trademarks used herein under license.

For more information, contact
Lucent Books
27500 Drake Rd.
Farmington Hills, MI 48331-3535
Or you can visit our Internet site at http://www.gale.com.

LIBRARY OF CONGRESS CATALOGING-IN-PUBLICATION DATA

Barter, James, 1946–
    Medieval Constantinople / by James Barter.
        p. cm. — (A travel guide to:)
    Summary: A visitor's guide to Constantinople in 1024, including what to see, where to
stay, and what to eat, with sidebars on such topics as Emperor Constantine, the Hagia
Sophia, and a drink made of roasted beans from Kaffa.
    Includes bibliographical references and index.
        ISBN 1-59018-249-9 (hardback : alk. paper)
        1. Istanbul (Turkey)—Juvenile literature. 2. Istanbul (Turkey)—Description and travel.
    3. Istanbul (Turkey)—Guidebooks. [1. Istanbul (Turkey)—Civilization.] I. Title. II. Series.
        DR723 .B37 2003
        949.61'8012—dc21
                                                                2002015475

Printed in the United States of America

Contents

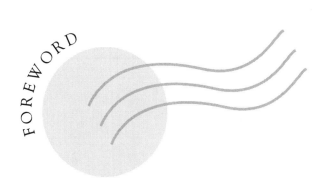

Travel can be a unique way to learn about oneself and other cultures. The esteemed American writer and historian, John Hope Franklin, poetically expressed his conviction in the value of travel by urging, "We must go beyond textbooks, go out into the bypaths and untrodden depths of the wilderness and travel and explore and tell the world the glories of our journey." The message communicated by this eloquent entreaty is clear: The value of travel is to temper one's imagination about a place and its people with reality, and instead of thinking how things may be, to be able to experience them as they really are.

Franklin's voice is not alone in his summons for students to "travel and explore." He is joined by a stentorian chorus of thinkers that includes former president John F. Kennedy, who established the Peace Corps to facilitate cross-cultural understandings between Americans and citizens of other lands. Ideas about the benefits of travel do not spring only from contemporary times. The ancient Greek historian Herodotus journeyed to foreign lands for the purpose of immersing himself in unfamiliar cultural traditions. In this way, he believed, he might gain a first-hand understanding of people and ways of life in other places.

The joys, insights, and satisfaction that travelers derive from their journeys are not limited to cultural understanding. Travel has the added value of enhancing the traveler's inner self by expanding his or her range of experiences. Writer Paul Tournier concurs that, "The real meaning of travel, like that of a conversation by the fireside, is the discovery of oneself through contact with other people."

The Lucent Books Travel Guide series enlivens history by introducing a new and innovative style and format. Each volume in the series presents the history of a preeminent historical travel destination written in the casual style and format of a travel guide. Whether providing a tour of fifth-century B.C. Athens, Renaissance Florence, or Shakespeare's London, each book describes a city or area at its cultural peak and orients readers to only those places and activities that are known to have existed at that time.

A high level of authenticity is achieved in the Travel Guide series. Each book is written in the present tense and addresses the reader as a prospective foreign traveler. The sense of authenticity is further achieved, whenever possible, by the inclusion of descriptive quotations by contemporary writers who knew the place; information on fascinating historical sites; and travel tips meant to explain unusual cultural idiosyncrasies that give depth and texture to all great cultural centers. Even shopping details, such as where to buy an ermine-trimmed gown, or a much-needed house slave, are included to inform readers of what items were sought after throughout history.

Looked at collectively, this series presents an appealing presentation of many of the cultural and social highlights of Western civilization. The collection also provides a framework for discussion about the larger historical currents that dominated not only each travel destination but countries and entire continents as well. Each book is customized by the author to bring to the fore the most important and most interesting characteristics that define each title. High standards of scholarship are assured in the series by the generous peppering of relevant quotes and extensive bibliographies. These tools provide readers a scholastic standard for their own research as well as a guide to direct them to other books, periodicals, and websites that will provide them greater breadth and detail.

The Queen of Cities

There are a handful of cities around the world that command the attention of all the others. Today, in the year 1024, Constantinople enjoys such a reputation. The city thrives in the midst of what international travelers and diplomats are calling the city's Golden Age. Never before has this world-renowned cosmopolitan center of government, culture, art, Christianity, and commerce enjoyed a longer period of peace and prosperity. Following troubled times caused by attacking Muslim armies, the city now celebrates an era of unprecedented tranquility, which began more than 150 years ago.

Constantinople flourishes under the brilliant leadership of Emperor Basil II. He is already acclaimed Constantinople's greatest emperor since Emperor Constantine himself, the city's namesake who moved the capital of the Roman Empire from Rome to our splendid metropolis seven hundred years ago. Since that dramatic historic decision, our population has swelled to 1 million people drawn from dozens of different nations, practicing several diverse religions, and speaking a multitude of languages. It comes as no surprise to Constantinopolitans that their city surpasses in size, wealth, and international charm its aging and worn-out predecessors: Rome, Athens, Moscow, Jerusalem, Alexandria, and Cairo. This is the best of times for sightseers and travelers to visit modern Constantinople, known among its predominantly Greek-speaking population as Βασιλευουσα, Queen of Cities.

This queen sits upon her throne at the crossroads of Europe and Asia, where the waters of the Bosphorus and the Golden Horn Estuary flow into the Sea of Marmara. No city, European or Asian, can lay claim to a more exquisitely beautiful setting or a better natural location for funneling people and trade from one culturally distinct continent to the other. Here cargo ships loaded to the gunwales and camel caravans plodding their way across the eastern deserts come to unload and sell their precious cargos.

A bounty of merchandise floods Constantinople's world-renowned marketplaces. Colorful and sweet-smelling spices, some worth more than their weight in gold, enhance the city's food, and handwoven wool carpets, years in the making and dyed in every imaginable color, grace the city's private homes. Mosaics of ceramics, jewels, and glass decorate the city's many Christian churches, while silk and leather, dyed and stitched into intricate clothing designs, create a colorful and flamboyant blur as their wearers hurry throughout the city's narrow, crowded streets. Along the city's great commercial avenues, pushcarts overflowing with gold, silver, and brass trinkets bump their way across the city's cobblestone streets with goods to decorate people, homes, and businesses.

Constantinople also provides a cornucopia of cultural offerings. No city displays greater magnificence in monumental architecture, churches, gardens, and harbors than does this grand city. Travelers approaching by boat are stunned as they stand at the ship's prow watching the city's landmarks gradually come into view. Everyone comments on the magnitude and elegance of the city's famous circuit defense walls, the numerous protected harbors that make the city a safe haven for ships of all sizes, the many church domes dominating the city's skyline, and the luxuriant architecture of the Imperial Palace and many ornate municipal buildings.

There has never been a better time to visit the Queen of Cities. Our remarkable conglomeration of different nationalities, diverse languages, distinctive clothing,

Constantinople, the Queen of Cities, is world renowned for its commerce and culture. More than 1 million people from many different nations live within its walls.

The formidable walls surrounding Constantinople have protected the city from invaders for many centuries.

and differing religions creates an unforgettable human scenery that blends and flows throughout the city's architectural scenery—which, in turn, enchances the city's natural scenery. Everyone will feel at home within such an unusual cultural convergence, just as an anonymous poet once observed many years ago, "Constantinople is a city not of one nation but of many, and hardly more of one than of another."[1]

CHAPTER ONE

A Brief History of Constantinople

Sixteen hundred years ago, in 633 B.C., a Greek adventurer named Byzas sailed northeast across the Aegean Sea from his home in Megara to find a new home for the colonists he led. As the small ship moved north, it sailed through the narrow channel of the Dardanelles, then into the open waters of the Sea of Marmara, and finally to the entrance of the Bosphorus. The Bosphorus (sometimes spelled Bosporus) is the narrow finger of water that snakes its way for twenty miles through rocky, desolate hills until emerging into the expansive Black Sea. This threadlike stretch of water barely a half mile across, which provided the most obvious crossing point for people and animals, took its name from the Greek words for cattle and crossing, *bos* and *phorous*.

Byzas landed his boatload of colonists on a beautiful triangular site along the west side of the Bosphorus. It provided natural defenses as well as a strategic location for trade between the Black Sea and the Mediterranean by boat, and for trade with Greece by land. Delighted with the ideal location, Byzas named the newly founded colony after himself, Byzantium; this was the name of the city for nine hundred years, until it was renamed Constantinople.

An ancient Greek story claims that before Byzas set sail from Megara, he walked from his home to the city of Delphi, the religious center of Greece, to consult the Delphic Oracle about his search for a new home. When he asked the priestess where he should search for a new colony, she answered, "opposite the blind." Not sure what might be meant by such a strange riddle, he set sail uncertain of his destination. It was only when he reached the Bosphorus that he understood the riddle. Opposite the triangular site on the west side of the Bosphorus that Byzas had chosen for a new city, earlier Greek colonists had founded the colony of Chalcedon (on the east side that did not have as desirable a location). It was the Chalcedonians, Byzas concluded, who must have been blind not to have noticed the superiority of the opposite shore for the founding of a great city.

Byzantium and the Greeks

Byzantium was a Greek colony, yet Greek writers, in a trend that continued for hundreds of years, had little to say about the city during Greece's Golden Age of the fifth century B.C. For most of this time, Greek historians largely focused on the events and affairs of the three great city-states of Athens, Sparta, and Corinth. And besides, Greek colonies could be found throughout the Mediterranean; most simply served to reduce population pressures in Greece, while providing Greek city-states with goods not available in the homeland. One small bit of history, however, suggests that the Chalcedonians and Byzantines apparently maintained amicable relationships: Both their names are found on coins that they jointly minted.

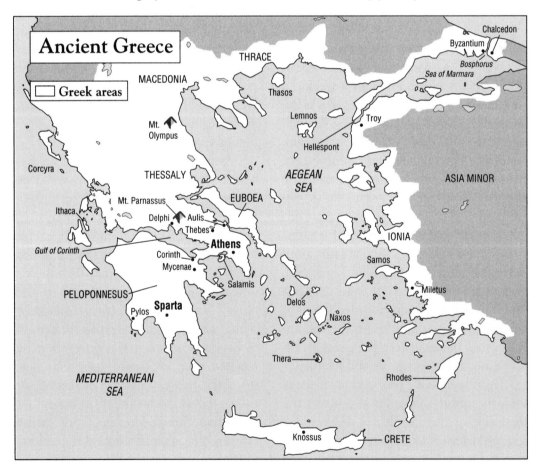

At some time, probably the third century B.C. when the city began expanding, a three-mile defense wall with twenty-seven watchtowers was built across the tip of the peninsula. Within the walls, near the Imperial Palace and today's chariot track called the Hippodrome, a few remnants of the ancient city can still be seen.

The growth of the city and its early inhabitants went unnoticed by the Roman Empire for many years. However, on a local level the city thrived. Revenues obtained from fishing, tolls paid by ships passing though the Bosphorus, and the fertility of the surrounding soil all contributed to the success of the city.

But by the second century B.C. the relative calm that had characterized the city ended. When Rome first became an imperial powerhouse and began expanding its grip first over Italy, then the western Mediterranean, and finally the eastern Mediterranean, Byzantium's ideal strategic location was noticed. What for centuries had been its greatest asset would soon become its greatest liability.

The Romans Seize Control

Byzantium's calm was shattered by the Romans. During the early 190s (A.D.), two Roman generals, Pescennius Niger and Septimius Severus, fought for control of the Roman Empire. Tragically for the citizens of Byzantium, the city supported the loser, Niger. His severed head was sent to Byzantium by Severus as a signal that the citizens would soon pay the price for their rash decision to support Niger.

In 194, the approaching sounds of tramping feet belonging to thousands of Rome's legions were heard at the city's walls. The siege of the city that ensued ended two years later when Byzantium finally surrendered and, in so doing, witnessed the slaughter of all its soldiers and politicians, the destruction of its walls, and the reduction of its legal status to that of a village. Severus, however (who continued to rule the empire until 211), understood the importance of the city's location and ordered the city rebuilt and even expanded.

Internal skirmishes between Roman political and military rivals continued to rack the empire. One hundred years following Severus, the empire was divided, east and west, between two emperors in an attempt to remedy its many problems. Although at first this seemed to be a reasonable solution to Rome's problems, the dual-emperor approach disintegrated into conflict until Emperor Constantine fought and defeated his fellow emperor, Maxentius, in 312.

Ruling without a rival, Constantine decided upon a course of action so dramatic and perilous that no great leader has ever again attempted such a turn of events. Constantine abandoned Rome as the seat of power for the Roman Empire in favor of Byzantium. In 330, eight hundred years after the founding of Rome, Constantine—followed by the Roman Senate, the aristocracy, military leaders, and all families supporting the government—departed the city, never to return.

13

Constantine's Conversion

The fame of Emperor Constantine stems not only from his founding of Constantinople as the seat of the Roman Empire but also from his apparent conversion from paganism to Christianity. The conversion seems to have occurred in 312 in Rome the night before Constantine fought Maxentius for control of the Roman Empire. As historians tell this remarkable story, Constantine had drawn up his army at the Milvian Bridge in anticipation of a great and decisive battle the next morning. When the sun rose, Constantine awoke and issued the order to his generals and soldiers that all must paint a cross on their shields to guarantee victory.

The two great armies clashed, and Constantine's army overwhelmed the other making Constantine the sole emperor in Rome. When asked why he had issued the order to paint the sign of the cross on all shields, he replied by telling about a dream that had come to him the previous night. He explained that while he slept a vision came displaying the cross and saying, "in hoc signo vinces," Latin for "in this sign you will conquer."

Following this famous dream and military victory, Constantine did many things that indicated his conversion to Christianity—although being a good diplomat, he did not completely abandon paganism, which was very popular in Rome. Nonetheless, many people, such as the fifth-century Christian thinker, Sozomen, believed that Constantine founded Constantinople as a statement of his newfound Christian faith—as he indicates in his Ecclesiastical History:

In a dream Emperor Constantine is told Christianity is the path to his success.

Led by the divine hand, he came to Byzantium in Thrace, beyond Chalcedon in Bithynia, and here he desired to build his city, and render it worthy of the name of Constantine. In obedience to the command of God, he therefore enlarged the city formerly called Byzantium, and surrounded it with high walls; likewise he built splendid dwelling houses; and being aware that the former population was not enough for so great a city, he peopled it with men of rank and their families, whom he summoned from Rome and from other countries. By the favor of God, it became the most populous and wealthy of cities.

Constantine's New Rome

Few historic decisions, if any, have been more momentous than Constantine's abandonment of the traditional capital. May 11, 330 marked the official celebration commemorating the founding of *Nova Roma*, New Rome. As Constantine entered the city, his supporters hailed him as *Constantinus Magnus*, Constantine the Great. Shortly after that, the city that had been known to the world as Byzantium for nine hundred years became *Urbs Constantini*, the City of Constantine or Constantinople, the name still in use to this day.

The location, superbly chosen nine hundred years earlier, was admirably suited for an imperial residence where Constantine could run his empire. He could keep an eye on the Persians, who were threatening the empire from the east, and on several Germanic tribes along the Danube that were always trying to break through Rome's northern boundaries.

The city had for many years supported Christianity, rather than the variety of non-Christian religions practiced in Rome. Many Roman historians, who wrote about the shift of government from Rome to Constantinople, believed that part of Constantine's decision to abandon Rome was based on his conversion to Christianity and a perceived need for a Christian city to be the new capital of the empire.

The new capital required expansion and elaboration to accommodate the thousands of new families needed to ad-

The profile of Constantine the Great graces Byzantine coins.

minister the empire. New homes were needed for the lower orders of administrators, villas were needed for the upper rungs of society, and a great palace was required for Constantine. Dozens of major administrative offices were constructed to accommodate law courts and the bureaucracies responsible for building roads, aqueducts, and defense walls. Marketplaces sprang up to feed the populace, as did structures for storing grain and several new harbors for the transfer of merchandise. To entertain the bulging population, Constantine built the Hippodrome, a giant arena capable of accommodating sixty thousand spectators who enjoyed the regularly scheduled chariot

A First-Century Description of Byzantium

The geography books written by the first-century A.D. traveler Strabo are old but remain a valuable source of geography and natural history for travelers. The following description can be found in his work, Geographika, *written two hundred years before Constantine christened Constantinople and so refers to the city and people as Byzantium and Byzantines:*

Now the distance from the headland that makes the strait only five stadia [one *stadium* equals one-eighth mile] wide to the harbor which is called "Under the Fig-tree" is thirty-five stadia; and thence to the Horn of the Byzantines, five stadia. The Horn, which is close to the wall of the Byzantines, is a gulf that extends approximately towards the west for a distance of sixty stadia; it resembles a stag's horn, for it is split into numerous gulfs—branches, as it were. The pelamydes [a local fish] rush into these gulfs and are easily caught—because of their numbers, the force of the current that drives them together, and the narrowness of the gulfs; in fact, because of the narrowness of the area, they are even caught by hand.

But the Chalcedonians, though situated nearby, on the opposite shore, have no share in this abundance, because the pelamydes do not approach their harbors; hence the saying that Apollo, when the men who founded Byzantium at a time subsequent to the founding of Chalcedon by the Megarians consulted the oracle, ordered them to "make their settlement opposite the blind," thus calling the Chalcedonians "blind," because, although they sailed the regions in question at an earlier time, they failed to take possession of the country on the far side, with all its wealth, and chose the poorer country. I have now carried my description as far as Byzantium, because a famous city, lying as it does very near to the mouth, marked a better-known limit to the coasting-voyage from the Ister [Danube River].

races. In addition, Constantine erected theaters for musical and theatrical performances. For relaxation, he built 8 enormous public baths, 150 private baths, and a large circular forum in the middle of the city where people could gather and casually enjoy the day or go about their personal business.

Symbols of Christianity also received Constantine's attention. He built fourteen churches to broadcast the message of his conversion to Christianity, including the crown jewel of the churches, Hagia Sophia. From throughout the Christian world he collected relics significant to the faithful. He gathered pieces reputed to have been bits of swaddling clothes worn by Jesus as a baby, a blood-stained piece of linen worn by Jesus on the cross, the crown of thorns, and the stone that blocked the entrance of Jesus' tomb (where he reposed until his resurrection).

To protect the greatly embellished city, Constantine built a new, much longer and stronger defense wall a mile and a half beyond the old walls built by Severus. The church historian Sozomen, writing about 450, made this observation about Constantine and his new city: "He . . . enlarged the city formerly called Byzantium, and surrounded it with high walls; likewise he built splendid dwelling houses. He erected all the needed edifices for a great capital—a hippodrome, fountains, porticoes and other beautiful adornments."[2]

On May, 22, 337, while traveling to Nicomedia, Constantine died. Many historians mourned the passing of the man they believed to be the most influential of the late Roman emperors. Constantine's work of relocating the seat of Roman power to Constantinople and the money he spent expanding, defending, and beautifying the city paid handsome dividends to its citizens for many generations.

From the death of Constantine until the reign of Justinian two hundred years later, Constantinople and the eastern half of the Roman Empire continued to expand

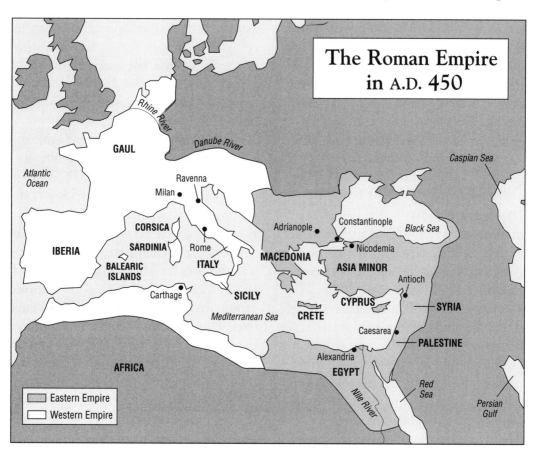

The Roman Empire in A.D. 450

Eastern Empire
Western Empire

and progress with remarkable energy. The same could not be said for Rome and the western half of the empire, which experienced contraction and decline. Wave after wave of German invaders sacked Rome, first in 410 and then one final devastating blow in 476, from which the Western Roman Empire never recovered.

Seeming unaffected by the collapse of old Rome and the western empire, young Constantinople looked forward to playing a dominant role in the future of the eastern empire. The walls that are visible today were built farther west and along the coast to accommodate the growing city, more aqueducts were built to quench the thirst of a growing population, and the continuing wave of citizens converting to Christianity spurred the construction of more elaborate churches throughout the city. The gleaming marble that for centuries had defined Rome had moved east to adorn the new capital.

Emperor Justinian to the Present

Emperor Justinian, who reigned from 518 to 565, is generally considered the last great emperor of either the western or eastern empire. His greatness was due to his ability to skillfully administer the eastern empire and keep enemies at bay while continuing the city's energetic building program begun by Constantine. His flare for building exquisite architecture was partially the result of a fire in 532 that raged unchecked throughout the city for five days. When it finally burned itself to the sea, half the city was in ruins and many of Constantine's architectural achievements lay smoldering in ashes.

The city that all vacationers see today is principally the result of Justinian's rebuilding efforts. Fortunately for everyone, Justinian immediately cleared the rubble and began the most ambitious construction program since Constantine's reign. He summoned the two most famous architects of the time, Isidore of Miletus and Anthemius of Tralles, to take charge of designing and rebuilding the city. Highest on his list of priorities was to rebuild the most venerated church in the city, Hagia Sophia, a project requiring six years to complete. In spite of many damaging earthquakes, this is the same Hagia Sophia still visited by thousands of devout worshippers today. It remains the crowning glory of the city.

Following Justinian's burst of enthusiasm for the revitalization of the city, many emperors and empresses ruled Constantinople and the eastern empire, but none continued his expansion and beautification program. The primary reason for the slowing of the expansion of the city was the Muslim threat. As followers of the prophet Muhammad, this religious group sought to expel all Christians from the eastern Mediterranean, and part of their expulsion plan was the capture of Constantinople. First in 673 and then again in 717, Muslim armies besieged the city, but each time the defending army and war fleet drove them off.

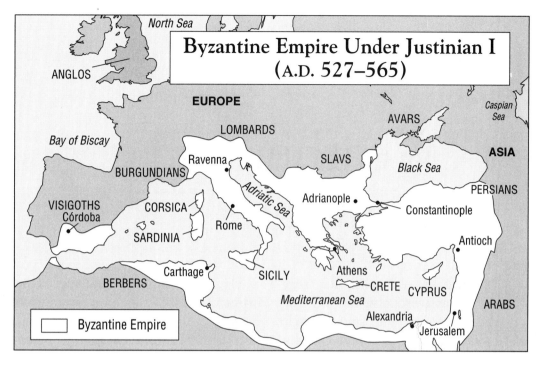

Byzantine Empire Under Justinian I
(A.D. 527–565)

Today the threat of further Muslim attacks is unimaginable. Since 867, the beginning of what is now called the Golden Age, the city has been fortunate to have the greatest continuous line of rulers in its history. Beginning with Basil I, a military genius; Leo VI, known for his great wisdom; Constantine VII, one of the great patrons of the arts; and continuing with today's emperor, Basil II, the succession of leaders has left the city prosperous and secure. In fact, Basil II, a brilliant general and statesman whose reign began in 976,

has now been on the throne for forty-eight years, and it is hoped he will continue to rule for a long time.

This is truly Constantinople's Golden Era. The Muslims have been pushed far from our city, providing visitors with safe entry routes. Constantinople is as dazzling as ever because the world's wealth pours in through trade routes from Russia to the north, Persia and India to the east, Egypt to the south, and Europe to the west. Only peace and prosperity seem on the horizon for the Queen of Cities.

CHAPTER TWO

Weather and Location

There is an old saying here that there are two climates in Constantinople: that of the north wind and that of the south wind. These winds create the seasonal differences between summer and winter and provide travelers to Constantinople with two seemingly different destinations depending on when they arrive.

Nothing changes the character and tempo of the city more than the seasons. Winters here—which bring temperatures ranging from the high thirties to the mid-fifties accompanied by no more than four inches of rain a month—will seem mild and will be welcomed by guests traveling from frigid northern locations such as Russia or snow-blanketed Northern European countries close to the North Sea (such as Germany and the Scandinavian countries). Visitors from southern cities, such as Rome, Athens, Baghdad, and Jerusalem, will find the temperatures a bit more chilly, but not too much different from those near their homes. There is no need to pack extra heavy clothing; in the event of a cold snap, Constantinople's marketplaces will be able to provide the latest fashions in cloaks and fur-lined overcoats.

Seasonal Offerings

Generally, winter weather does not restrict out-of-door tourist activities because rains rarely last more than a few hours and freezing temperatures are unheard of. This is especially appreciated by travelers coming down the Danube River because their boats can easily reach the Black Sea and then continue south to our city without encountering ice. Besides, one of the city's greatest attractions is its art and architecture, providing comfortable indoor cultural experiences.

Although there is much to be enjoyed inside the art galleries and grand churches, it is not until temperatures begin to warm into the seventies that out-of-door activities begin to spring to life, and owners of open-air markets unfurl their colorful canopies to display their wares. It was the great traveler Benjamin of Tudela who, after recently visiting Constantinople, observed in his book, *The Itinerary of Benjamin of Tudela*, "It is a busy city, and merchants come to it from every country by sea or land, and there is none like it in the world except Baghdad, the great city of Islam."[3]

Temperatures in the summer warm to a very comfortable range between seventy and eighty degrees under clear, sunny skies, and rain trails off to about an inch and a half between April and September. As the temperature improves, all outdoor activities come to life, and the city's population swells with a tremendous influx of foreign visitors. No matter which season you choose, the climate of our city is both healthy and relaxing.

In addition to tourists who make Constantinople their sole destination, many Christians from Europe make the city a stopping place on their way to and from the Holy Land in general and Jerusalem in particular. Ever since our armies drove the Muslims out of the sacred city, more Christian travelers have taken an interest in visiting Jerusalem and using Constantinople as a colorful and culturally stimulating halfway point.

The Crossroads of Europe and Asia

Geography is the heart and soul of Constantinople's greatness. No other single characteristic can account for its international prominence. The city sits at the crossroads of Europe and Asia, a dominating location unsurpassed by any other city on either continent. Today this location is

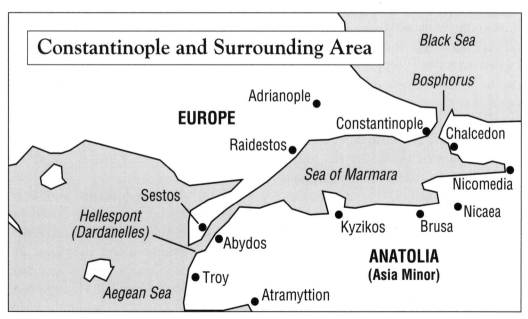

Constantinople and Surrounding Area

of far greater strategic importance than it was when founded by Byzas.

Locating Constantinople on a map will be an easy task for travelers with access to one. A useful book that provides maps as well as descriptions of towns is *Expositio Totius Mundi et Gentium*. But if a copy is not available, an excellent source combining geography with ethnography is a set of three small books titled *Geographika*, by the Greek writer Strabo. Yet another more recent travel book that includes maps is the work of the sixth-century Alexandrian merchant Cosmas Indicopleustes.

Although a few maps of the area are available, they are drawn with ink on vellum (the cleaned and dried skins of goats and sheep) and are a rare commodity typically available only to the very rich, monastic scholars, sea captains who trade with our city, and military leaders who must know the detailed topography of the region. Although the city's fame has fanned out across Europe and Asia for the past five hundred years, most travelers are not able to consult a map.

For those without a map, Constantinople is located at the tip of a peninsula, shaped somewhat like a triangle, jutting into the water at the southernmost point of the Bosphorus. This tip commands and controls all north-south shipping that passes through the narrow Bosphorus, moving back and forth between ports throughout the Black Sea and the Mediterranean Sea. This channel is Russia's only shipping lane that does not freeze solid during the winter, making it the only direct channel to commercial markets throughout Europe and the Middle East.

Constantinople also controls all east-west land caravans of horses and camels, wagon trains, foot travelers, and armies that cross the Bosphorus as they make their way to and from Europe and Asia. Although other land routes are available, all of them either lead hundreds of miles to the north around the Black Sea (second in size to only the Mediterranean) or south hundreds of miles into Egypt and North Africa. Anyone seeking a direct route between Europe and Asia and wishing to avoid ships must pass across the narrow Bosphorus.

For more than a thousand years, this location has functioned as an economic funnel attracting tens of thousands of ships and caravans from dozens of countries and hundreds of exotic far-off cities. This site makes Constantinople the most alluring commercial center in all of Europe and Asia; rare and exotic goods pour into the city. It also makes Constantinople one of the word's wealthiest cities because each cargo ship and caravan wishing to pass must pay a toll or be turned back.

On any day, the docks and warehouses of Constantinople receive and disperse mountains of the world's most extraordinary merchandise. These shipments include: aromatic spices from points east; beautifully grained timber for expensive furniture; thick, lustrous furs for the coats of stately men and women; scented wax for the millions of candles that illuminate the city's churches; mosaic art for everyone's enjoyment; brass house ornaments; silk fabrics not found elsewhere in the world; "magical" Persian carpets; fruits and vegetables grown only in the Mediterranean's favorable climate; and Slavic slaves to care for the homes and personal needs of the rich.

The Golden Horn

As an added bonus to being situated at the intersection of major land and sea routes, Constantinople has an estuary that provides an excellent harbor to shelter the hundreds of ships that arrive each month. This five-mile-long estuary along the north border of the city is formed in the shape of a horn and is known to the locals as the

The estuary called the Golden Horn separates Christian, commercial Constantinople from the non-Christian, industrial district called Galata.

Golden Horn. The estuary plays a major role in the commercial life of the city because it provides one of the best natural harbors in the world to facilitate the loading and unloading of cargo. The great historian Procopius recognized the significance of the Golden Horn for shipping in the sixth century when he observed:

The Horn is always calm, being made by nature never to be stormy, as though limits were set to the billows and the surge was shut out in the city's honor. And in winter when harsh winds fall upon the sea and the strait [the Bosphorus], as soon as ships reach the bay's entrance, they can proceed without pilot and moor easily.[4]

The Golden Horn also serves as a watery barrier separating one district of the city from the rest. The one isolated district, called Galata, has for centuries provided a location for all undesirable businesses—such as slaughterhouses, tanneries, and fish processing houses engaged in smelly and disgusting activities. The location of these businesses, away from the

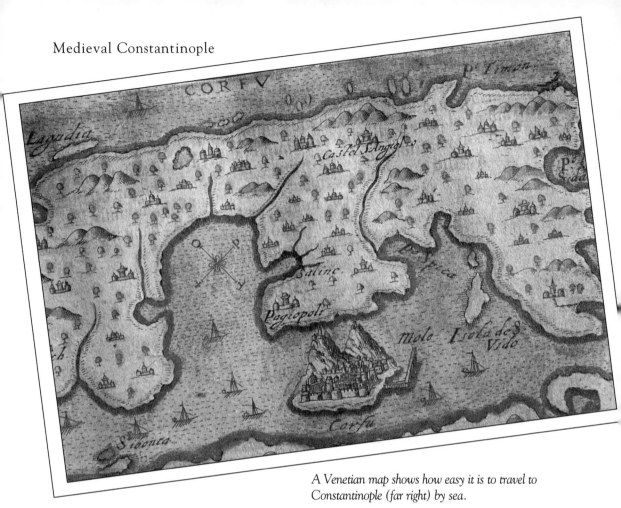

A Venetian map shows how easy it is to travel to Constantinople (far right) by sea.

rest of the city, is partially successful at keeping the foul odors that emanate from them away from the rest of the city. The estuary also functions successfully as a sewer; blood and nonedible, discarded animal parts are removed by its daily flushing action.

The Golden Horn also separates non-Christian elements from the rest of the city. Populations of Muslims and Jews, although allowed to carry out their business in all districts of Constantinople during the day, must return to their homes in Galata by nightfall.

Traveling to Constantinople

Fortunately for everyone planning to visit Constantinople, several well-established land and sea routes have been used by generations of travelers and are known to ship captains and caravan organizers. The decision to travel by land or by sea will depend upon travelers' points of departure and their finances. In some cases, a combination of both modes of travel may be the most expedient.

Most land routes from Europe to Constantinople remain roads built by Roman legions during the first, second,

Roman Roads

The ancient Romans had a good system of roads, one which required systematic planning and maintenance. When planning the path that a road would take, Roman engineers sought the easiest route, avoiding tunnels, steep inclines, and bridges whenever possible. Once the most expeditious route was defined, hordes of workers, often soldiers without wars to fight, set to work.

Proper drainage is crucial for roads to protect them from being undermined and washed away during heavy rains and floods. To aid drainage, drains with a slight slope were dug on either side of the proposed route and filled with rock and gravel to capture and divert water from the road. Between the two drains, workers using picks and shovels dug down between two and five feet the entire width of the proposed road, which could range anywhere between ten and forty feet.

The key to the finished road was the layers of aggregate that were first laid down into the road trench. The first layer was rubble, broken pieces of large stone that would solidify the entire road and drain off any water that soaked to the bottom. The middle section consisted of several thinner layers of sand, gravel, and clay. On top of this was the final layer of heavy basalt blocks or similar heavy stones. These flat stones were tamped down with thick, heavy timbers to set them firmly in place. Occasionally, but not often, a concrete grout was placed in the spaces between the top layer stones. The grout prevented those stones from shifting under the weight of heavy wagons and acted as a waterproofing agent that prevented water from seeping down.

Many of the Roman roads between Rome and Constantinople have been in continuous use for more than one thousand years, a testimony to the high quality of Roman engineering, building materials, and laborers.

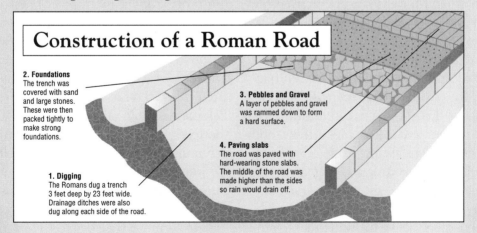

Construction of a Roman Road

2. Foundations
The trench was covered with sand and large stones. These were then packed tightly to make strong foundations.

3. Pebbles and Gravel
A layer of pebbles and gravel was rammed down to form a hard surface.

4. Paving slabs
The road was paved with hard-wearing stone slabs. The middle of the road was made higher than the sides so rain would drain off.

1. Digging
The Romans dug a trench 3 feet deep by 23 feet wide. Drainage ditches were also dug along each side of the road.

and third centuries A.D. Although old, these roads remain some of the best because many were expertly built of six- to eight-inch-thick basalt blocks set in a deep substratum made of sand and crushed gravel. Over the years, the roads have remained intact and perhaps even improved; the wheels of thousands of wagons and chariots have worn grooves that now minimize the banging and clattering of the wagon wheels of modern travelers.

Travel will be slow whether on horseback or by horse-drawn wagon. But the popularity of travel to Constantinople has stimulated the growth of inns along major routes that will provide comfortable accommodations for the night, including livery service for horses and hearty meals for travelers. There are, of course, inherent dangers on the road, especially from thieves, and for that reason most travelers nowadays travel in organized caravans for mutual protection.

The difficulties, dangers, and exhaustion of land travel motivate most people venturing to Constantinople to do so by boat. Sea routes, both those traversing the open waters of the Mediterranean and those leapfrogging small islands while hugging the coastline, have been used for centuries, and boat captains carrying travelers know them well. Most ships arriving and departing Constantinople are oceangoing freighters transporting commercial goods, but a few, called cogs, are constructed to carry a small number of passengers in cabins built high above the waterline (to provide protection from the wet and cold).

These ships have a single mast and are capable of ten knots in a good wind. But most average only four to five knots and generally sail only during the day and close to land, to avoid the dangers of the open sea. As the sailor Theophylaktos explains, "We prefer sailing along the coast, touching the land with our oars."[5] Travelers coming to Constantinople from the island of Cyprus can anticipate a ten-day trip; from Athens, six days; from Cairo or Rome, fifteen days; and from Venice, eighteen. Port cities along the route have developed a thriving industry providing a wide variety of warm and comfortable inns that guarantee a good night's rest and hot meals.

The Rhodian Maritime Law, which governs all ships approaching or departing Constantinople, specifies certain onboard conditions for passengers. Men, for example, must be provided cabins with at least sixty square feet of space and women one third that of a man. Passengers are forbidden from chopping wood for fires or frying fish on board, but the captain must provide water for passengers and a small canteen to feed them.

Vessels bound for Constantinople from Europe avoid the long and dangerous circuit down and around the Greek Peloponnese by taking an interesting shortcut. Instead of going around that peninsula, ships pass through the Gulf of Corinth and are then hauled across the three-and-one-half-mile-wide Isthmus of Corinth and deposited in the Saronic Gulf to continue their voyage. They then sail north, zigzagging through the Greek

Stopping at Meteora

One of the advantages of traveling to Constantinople by land is the opportunity to stop and visit many unusual sites. Perhaps the most remarkable that travelers will find in central Greece is the monastic community of Meteora. Perched high atop spires of rock jutting a thousand feet above the valley below, the monasteries of Meteora make it one of the world's most spectacular sacred sites. The word Meteora in Greek means "hovering in air." Allocating a day to visit one or two of these architectural and cultural early-Christian treasures will prove to be a rewarding decision.

Only men may visit this isolated monastery where monks devote themselves to silence, solitude, and prayer.

The arrival of Christianity in the region began in the eighth century when monks wishing to lead lives of ascetic devotion arrived and lived in the isolation of caves. In time, they built these remarkable monasteries balanced on rocky peaks. All materials for construction, even the water for concrete and stucco, had to be hauled up in baskets, which are still the only means for accessing these centers of scholarship and art. To this day, the monks lead lives renouncing all physical comforts in favor of focusing their time and energy on prayer and worship.

Travelers stopping here may visit only if they are men. The monks take their vows of asceticism so seriously that they will not even allow female cats within their monasteries. To request a visit, find the basket suspended by a rope and pull on it. This will ring a bell high up in the monastery. If the monks wish to admit you, a signal will be given to jump into the basket and be hoisted up. Once on top, take time to appreciate the simplicity of monastic life, the beauty of the monks' mosaic artwork, and their exquisitely painted manuscripts. Share a simple meal with the brethren of bread, olive oil, and grain, but do not expect meat, wine, or pastries. Remember to be respectful of their vows of silence and commitment to solitude and prayer.

islands until reaching the fortified point of Abydus on the Hellespont, where all stop and pay customs dues.

Just as is the case with land travel, ships are occasionally attacked. Ship captains are wary of pirates that infest the coastline of the eastern Mediterranean and prefer to travel in convoys. Yet, as the world traveler Daniel of Russia learned, safety is not a guarantee on land or sea. Of his journey, Daniel wrote:

We passed many towns without landing, and, for fear of the armed men, did not cast anchor at Khilidonia. From thence we proceeded towards Myra,

Crossing the Isthmus of Corinth

Travel from Europe to Constantinople by ship can become a tedious experience. Unpredictable winds and currents can slow travel and the nightly stops, although necessary for a good meal and night's rest, can slow the journey considerably. One experience that will break up the monotony of the voyage for travelers from Italy, France, and Spain is the crossing of the Isthmus of Corinth (separating the Gulf of Corinth on the west from the Saronic Gulf to the east).

This isthmus, a narrow and fairly low-lying three-and-a-half-mile tongue of land, links Central Greece and the Peloponnesus. Cutting across this spit of land to avoid sailing around the Peloponnesus cuts travel time by four to five days. Hundreds of years ago both the Greeks and Romans drew up plans to cut a canal through the isthmus, but complications prevented its completion.

Today, as passenger ships approach the isthmus, the captain will order all passengers to grab their personal belongings and prepare to disembark. As the ship pulls up along the south shore of the Gulf of Corinth, sails are furled, oars withdrawn into the ship, and as it hits the mud, the boat will slow to a stop and then dramatically list to one side. Planks are laid for passengers to depart the ship to awaiting wagons that will carry them across to the Saronic Gulf where their ship, after being moved overland, will then take them on their way.

The sight of the ship being dragged across the isthmus is quite a spectacle. Ropes are lashed to the ship and large wood rollers, made from entire tree trunks, are laid out in front of the ship. Teams of oxen—as many as twenty—strain at their leather harnesses to pull the ship from the mud and over the tree-trunk rollers. Once the ship starts its journey, workmen scurry to grab the rollers from behind the ship and run them ahead, laying them in the path of the ship. As this process continues, the ship gradually makes its way across the isthmus to the Saronic Gulf, shortening the delay from five days to five hours.

and also towards the town of Patara; near the latter we met four galleys, carrying pirates, who attacked and robbed us. From thence we directed our way towards Constantinople, which we reached in good health.[6]

Most piracy occurs along the east coast of the eastern Mediterranean and around the island of Cyprus, far from the route of European ships. Fortunately for Europeans, whose ships thread their way through the Greek islands, Constantinople sends out fleets of fast warships to protect these vital shipping lanes, making the approach to Constantinople the safest and most reliable in the Mediterranean.

First Glimpse of the City

European travelers approaching this splendid jewel by sea will glimpse the city's landmarks when they arrive at the junction where the waters of the Bosphorus and the Golden Horn flow into the Sea of Marmara. Such a nautical approach is an unforgettable experience. Travelers rush to the prow of their ship and crowd the rails to enjoy this most dramatic leg of their long journey—the moment their ship first comes into view of Constantinople. Although still a speck in the distance, Constantinople can be undeniably identified by the gleam of sunlight reflecting off its monuments.

Travelers' first good glimpse of our city occurs four or five miles to the south of the city as ships work their way up the Sea of Marmara toward the narrows of the Bosphorus, just off to the right of the ship. As the boat approaches, the city's southern coastal defensive wall will snap into focus, followed—just slightly off to the right—by the city's most commanding architectural treasure, the Church of Hagia Sophia. This splendid monument—the largest church in the world—sits atop the Acropolis, the highest hill on the extreme eastern tip of the peninsula. Rising two hundred feet above the base of the Acropolis, the reddish hue of the church's dome, with forty arched windows around its perimeter, presents a commanding sight. As Hagia Sophia looms larger, several tall, imperial marble columns, built to commemorate the city's great emperors, will come into view. They punctuate the city's skyline as the ship proceeds within a mile of the seawalls and protected harbors.

If your boat should arrive as the sun is setting, the arrival will be all the more dramatic because the fire in the lighthouse, which is along the same line of sight as Hagia Sophia, will be set. This navigational aid illuminates the evening sky and blazes until sunrise. Just in front of the lighthouse, the small harbor of Bukoleon comes into view. It is at this point that all ship captains will change course slightly to the west to enter one of three larger harbors: Eleutherius, Contoscalion, or Julian. All captains tack to the left because the harbor of Bukoleon, at starboard, is reserved exclusively for use by the royal family, and any ship attempting to enter will be intercepted by warships patrolling this area.

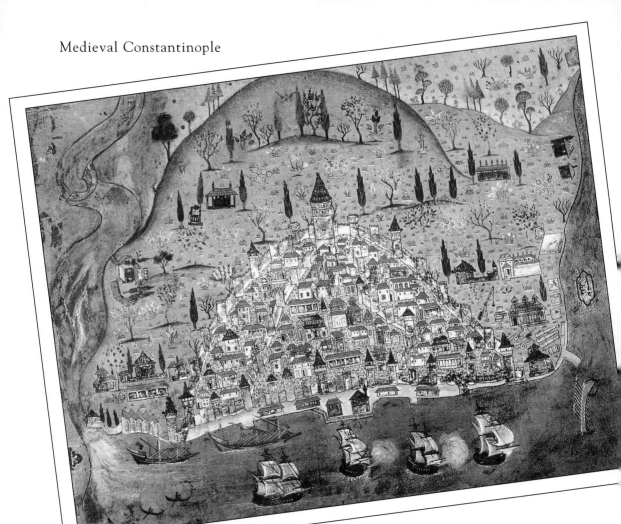

Fast warships keep Constantinople's shipping lanes free from pirates.

Travelers from Russia or northeastern Europe arriving by way of the Black Sea will enjoy a different yet equally breathtaking arrival. Heading south through the narrow Bosphorus, the view of Constantinople suddenly and dramatically appears to the right the moment the ship exits the strait into the open waters of the Sea of Marmara.

Immediately to the right on this course, ships sail to the entry of the Golden Horn and make a quick right turn toward one of several safe harbors. As the ships swing hard to the right, details of the seawall are easily identified, but everyone's eyes are then immediately drawn to the dome of Hagia Sophia, slightly to the left. As the ship moves up the Golden Horn, with Constantinople on the left, the one district of Constantinople that sits across the Golden Horn, Galata, comes into view. Most ships will then make a quick turn into the largest protected harbor on the city's north side, Phosphorion Harbor.

Whether arriving by boat from Europe, the eastern Mediterranean, or Russia, everyone will disembark at one of several harbors and enter the city through one of several gates. The gates are guarded by a small detail of guards but are open twenty-four hours a day as Constantinople's many decades of continuous peace no longer necessitate locking the gates at night.

Arriving and Becoming Familiar with the City

The first view within the walls will create a lasting impression. Most likely, the diversity of the population will be most impressive. The 1 million people who throng the city streets, most of whom are citizens of Constantinople, are also citizens of the world. Persians wearing turbans, bearded Jews from Palestine and Jerusalem, Bulgarians with closely cropped heads, Egyptians wearing tunics, and light-skinned and blue-eyed Scandinavians mix with the old Greek families as they hurry about their business. This melting pot of European and Asian peoples adds to the city's charm and unique character, making it truly cosmopolitan.

Newly arrived passengers are free to move about the city without any restrictions during daylight hours. However, at sunset the law dictates that, for the protection of all visitors and citizens, "A permanent curfew is enforced by armed men stationed at cross streets and squares where two, three, or four roads meet."[7]

The curfew is taken seriously, but no travelers need worry about arriving after curfew. Ship captains are aware of the law and schedule passages to arrive with plenty of time to allow passengers to find their ways to homes and inns.

Before wandering too far, travelers should first stop to exchange their money for the local currency so they can immediately purchase something to eat or pay for their lodgings, carriages, or boat taxis.

Exchanging Money

One of the benefits that Constantinopolitans derive from living in the largest, wealthiest, and most influential city within the Mediterranean basin is the tight control that the city exercises over coinage. Dozens of metropolitan centers strike their own coins made of gold, silver, and bronze, but only those struck in Constantinople are recognized and accepted without question throughout Europe and Asia. The trustworthiness of our coinage derives from generations of minting coins of precise weight and purity that has never been compromised over many years. As a result of the city's sterling reputation, all merchants, bankers, and foreign governments have learned to trust our coins. As the Egyptian merchant Cosmas Indicopleustes attests:

> There is yet another sign of the power which God has accorded to the people of Constantinople, to wit, that it is with their coinage that all nations do their trade: it is received everywhere from one end of the earth to the other: it is admired by all men and every kingdom, for no other kingdom has its like.[8]

Once travelers arrive, it is advised they go directly to one of the many banks to exchange foreign coins for those used in the city. Although local merchants will generally accept foreign denominations of gold and silver coins, they will not necessarily agree to the most favorable exchange rate (which banks will guarantee). This is especially true for shoppers who make purchases in one of the many marketplaces throughout the city that are not tightly controlled by city officials.

The coin most sought after, most valuable, and the basis for our economy is the gold coin called the *nomis-*

ma. This coin is commonly called the *solidus* within the walls of the city but a *bezant* elsewhere. From the time of Constantine the Great, the weight of the *nomisma* was set at precisely 4.48 grams of pure 24-carat gold. The beauty and prestige of this gold coin throughout the eastern Mediterranean is evident from the commonly heard compliment paid to attractive ladies. Such women are often described as being, "As beautiful and pure as a *bezant*."[9] Along with its beauty, the coin has an exceptional value. A middle-income worker does well to earn one *solidus* a month.

Following the *solidus* in value are the gold *tremissis*, called *triens* for short among local merchants. There are three *triens*

A solidus *minted during the reign of Byzantine emperor Arcadius.*

to one *solidus*. The most commonly exchanged silver coin is the *seliqua* weighing 2.24 grams. There are twenty-four *seliqua* to the *solidus* or eight to the *tremissis*. Since all of the gold and silver coins are considered quite valuable, the copper coin called the *folleis* is used for small purchases (there are twelve to the *seliqua*).

Of all the currency, the gold coins are works of art. Each is carefully hammered using precisely crafted iron coin die, or molds. Typically on one side of the coin, the portrait of the emperor or empress is presented in a frontal pose wearing a crown or diadem and holding a scepter; his or her name is located either at the bottom or around the outer perimeter. On the opposite side of the coin are found various Christian symbols such as the cross. Many Constantinopolitans fond of Emperor Basil II drill a hole in the *solidus* bearing his image and attach it to a leather cord for use as a necklace.

Speaking Greek

After monetary concerns are settled, foreigners making their first trip to Constantinople will probably want to consider how best to communicate in a city so culturally diverse. Within the walls of Constantinople, travelers are likely to hear more languages than they ever imagined existed. Part of the city's excitement and flair stems from its melting pot of heterogeneous elements, including all seventy-two languages presently known to exist. This many tongues heard simultaneously creates a cacophony of seemingly never-

Greek is the official language of Constantinople. Even bakers use Greek script to identify their product, as this bread stamp demonstrates.

Convenient Greek Phrases

Everyone vacationing in Constantinople who is not fluent in Greek will greatly enhance his or her visit to the city by knowing a few of the commonly used phrases. Knowing a few phrases will remove some of the uncertainty of spending money and reading signs to the city's many attractions as well as restaurant menus. This list of words and phrases, followed by phonetic pronunciations, will make your visit more memorable:

Good morning	Καλημερα	Kalimera
Good evening	Καλησπερα	Kalispera
Goodbye	Αντιο	Antio
Thank you	Ευχαριστω	Efharisto
Please	Παρακαλω	Parakalo
How are you	Τι κανετε	Ti kanete
Where is . . .	Που ειναι . . .	Poo ene . . .
I'm hungry	Θελω κατι να φαω	Thelo kate na fao
I would like a glass of water	Θελω Ενα ποταρι Νερο	Thelo Ena poteri nero
I would like bread	Θελω ψωμι	Thelo psomi
I would like fish	Θελω ψαρι	Thelo psari
I would like lamb	Θελω Αρνακι	Thelo arnake
I would like chicken	Θελω Κοτοπουλο	Thelo kotopoulo
I would like squid	Θελω Οχταποδι	Thelo okhtapothe
Do you have a hotel room	Εχετε ενα δωμαγιο	Ekhete ena thomateo
How much does this cost	Ποσο κοστιζει αυτο	Poso kosteze afto

ending babble down the streets and within the marketplaces throughout the city. Located at the crossroads of Europe and Asia, Constantinople boasts the most diverse population of any cosmopolitan center. Here first-time visitors will hear the distinct sounds of several Latin-based European languages, all Scandinavian and Slavic languages, Persian, Arabic, Egyptian, Hebrew, as well as many more from the lands of distant India and Egypt.

Although it might appear to casual tourists that any language will suffice, the official language of the city, and the one most often spoken and written, is Greek. Even though Emperor Constantine moved here from Rome when the language used throughout the Roman Empire was Latin, Constantinopolitans have always traced their cultural identity and traditions to Athens and other Greek cities that flourished during Greece's Golden Age in the fifth century B.C. Few Constantinopolitans would forget that their historical roots run back to Byzas and the early Greek settlement of the region.

Local merchants, hotel owners, and restaurateurs typically speak a smattering of several languages but will appreciate an effort on the part of travelers if they try a little Greek. In fact, travelers are advised, as a gesture of respect for the revered language, to learn enough Greek to greet people and to thank them for services. This may seem odd to some travelers, but it is important to recognize that most Greeks consider their language the most important element defining their culture. To a Greek, his language is superior to all others in terms of its euphony as well as its grammatical complexity that affords precise expression.

Greek speakers here are especially proud of their language's long history of use by great Greek thinkers and writers such as Homer, Aristotle, Socrates, Aeschylus, Sophocles, and Herodotus. Besides, learning the Greek alphabet—which is decidedly different from the Latin alphabet—will assist tourists in reading street signs and gaily colored banners announcing civic events or goods for sale in merchants' shops.

The Rhythm of the City

Constantinople is a great city for people who like to explore. Walking is a breeze because the city is relatively flat—with the sole exception of the low hill called the Acropolis occupied by the Church of Hagia Sophia. The pleasures of exploration are further heightened by the ocean on three sides that lends a unique beauty to the city as well as distant vistas over to the Asian continent. The city is also logically organized into fourteen districts, just like Rome. So, before venturing out into the city, here are a few helpful bits of information that explain the rhythm of the city to make everyone's visit the safest and most enjoyable possible.

Knowing the location of a few of the more interesting districts for tourism will speed one's journey and help locate the most direct route when asking for directions. Each of the districts has both a number and a name. Most locals use the names, so it is a good idea to know some of them. The numbers, however, are often more useful because they conform to a grid that makes determining one's location quite easy. The numbers were assigned by Emperor Constantine in a logical, sequential order beginning at the most eastern point of the city. Districts one through five, for example, occupy the eastern tip where the three main bodies of water meet. The district numbers then increase as the city spreads to the west. As a quick reminder, these first five districts will be of particular interest to first-time visitors because the three most visited and most loved architectural gems—the Hippodrome, the Sacred Imperial Palace, and the Church of Hagia Sophia—can be found within them. Should you become temporarily lost, however, you will not lack for help. There are men and boys everywhere who will offer to guide you to your destination for a *folleis* or two. Be aware, though, that these guides will seize the opportunity to sell you some trinket or ware as they direct you through the streets.

Knowing how to get around the city is as important as knowing where to find the major attractions. Constantinople's good fortune to be situated on a peninsula jutting into the water provides travelers with a choice of traversing the city by water or by streets. Although roads will generally be more direct and cheaper, boats are often faster, certainly quieter, and usually more comfortable.

Water taxis are available for hire at all of the city's small, protected harbors and at some of the gates along the wharves that line three of the city's four sides. During daylight hours, when the gates are open along the seawalls, anyone interested in traveling to any of the other harbors need only wander to the docks and hail a water taxi. The prices are set by the government so there is no need to worry about being cheated. A trip from the south side, from the harbor of Eleutherius, for example, all the way around the peninsula to the northside harbor of Phosphorion, will cost six *folleis*, if

Things to see in Constantinople include the Hippodrome (left), the Sacred Imperial Palace (right background), and the Church of Hagia Sophia (right foreground).

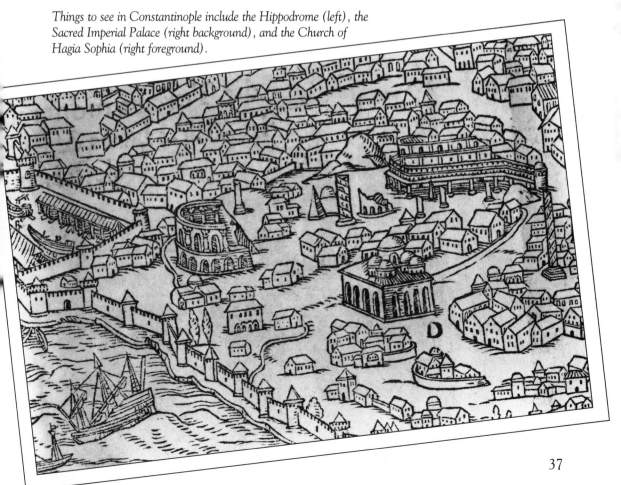

sharing the boat with other riders, or one *seliqua* for a private ride.

Mesê Street

Early city planners designed the city's streets to facilitate the comings and goings of large crowds to and from the major sites of interest, a plus for those with queasy stomachs. The major artery that moves throngs of people, horse-drawn carts, camels, and pushcarts to and from all major centers is Mesê Street, meaning Middle Street; the signs in Greek will look like this: οδός μέσος.

As long as everyone knows how to find this colorful and lively street, no one

should ever be lost for more than a moment. Mesê is the shape of a "Y" that starts at two gates at the city's wall: the Gate of Pegê to the south and the Gate of Charisius to the north. These two avenues head east, meeting at the Amastrian Forum where the single street continues to the major attractions until reaching the harbor at the Bosphorus.

Mesê Street was designed to function as the city's backbone for travel. Connecting to this street are hundreds of smaller ones creating a network crisscrossing the city that connects all districts and local neighborhoods. Many of the streets are indeed narrow. Most were built

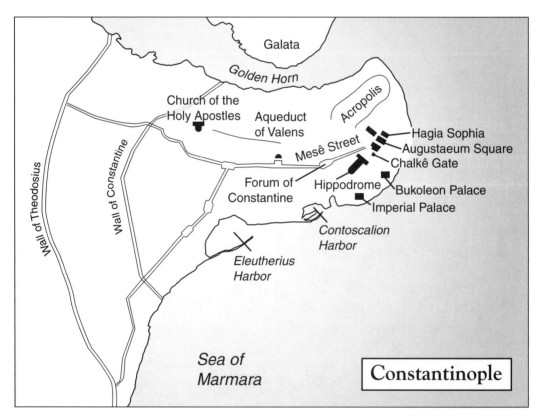

District Thirteen

Constantinople is a safe city and visitors are encouraged to wander wherever they like. Guards are usually not far away in the event of a mishap, and the ecumenical nature of the city makes for an enjoyable stay for visitors. The only cautionary note is in regard to the district of Galata, number thirteen, separated from the rest of the city by the Golden Horn. Avoiding this district is a matter of choice, not because of personal danger but rather because this is the district where the Jews and Muslims are required to settle by law. Because their religious opinions are theologically at odds with the Christian population, in the city proper the Jews and Muslims live isolated in district thirteen. When Benjamin of Tudela visited here he wrote in his book, The Itinerary of Benjamin of Tudela, *this description of Galata:*

No Jews live in the city, for they have been placed behind an inlet of the sea. An arm of the sea of Marmora shuts them in on the one side, and they are unable to go out except by way of the sea, when they want to do business with the inhabitants. In the Jewish quarter are about 2,000 Rabbanite Jews and about 500 Karaites [Jews who live according to the Hebrew Bible alone, not the oral Torah of the rabbinic tradition], and a fence divides them. Amongst the scholars are several wise men, at their head being the chief rabbi R. Abtalion, R. Obadiah, R. Aaron Bechor Shoro, R. Joseph Shir-Guru, and R. Eliakim, the warden. And amongst them there are artificers in silk and many rich merchants. No Jew there is allowed to ride on horseback. The one exception is R. Solomon Hamitari, who is the king's physician, and through whom the Jews enjoy considerable alleviation of their oppression. For their condition is very low, and there is much hatred against them, which is fostered by the tanners, who throw out their dirty water in the streets before the doors of the Jewish houses and defile the Jews' quarter. Yet the Jews are rich and good, kindly and charitable, and bear their lot with cheerfulness.

following the great fire of 532 that destroyed most of the city. Although donkey carts can squeeze down the streets, there is rarely enough room for two to pass at the same time. Do not be surprised to see products being hurried to markets on the backs of donkeys, camels, and even men bent over at the waist straining under a load equal to their own weight.

Fortunately for sightseers, in addition to Mesê Street, several other secondary thoroughfares are available and wide enough to accommodate large crowds. Many of these cut through the city funneling the throngs to the major marketplaces, gates, and city attractions.

Finding Lodging

With money in your pocket and a little knowledge about the Greek language, it is time to find lodging. Reasonably priced inns are available in all of the city's fourteen districts. Signs for inns will be in Greek and will appear like this: ζενοδοχείο. The prices for rooms are determined by their location, amenities, and views. The most economical rooms are found in the thirteenth district, Galata, located across the Golden Horn. It is the only district isolated from the rest of the city, and it is the only district where visiting Jews and Muslims are permitted to rent lodgings.

For all others, the least expensive inns are out along the city's land wall on the west edge of town. Expect to pay between six and ten *folleis* per night without meals. The most expensive inns, as is the case in many cities, are at the east end, close to the city's major attractions, where the costs can run between several *tremissi* to as high as one *solidus* per night.

The better rooms in inns are always in the upper stories of buildings, far from the noise, congestion, and smells of the streets. These better rooms will have small windows for fresh summer air and iron warming pans filled with hot charcoal to offset the effects of the cold and dampness of winter. Beds for the affluent traveler will have a rope mattress that requires lacing and tightening each evening. To reduce the discomfort of the ropes, a sheepskin is often first placed on the ropes, followed by two mattresses stuffed with goose down, and finally linen sheets. In the corner of the room guests will find a table and chair, and bronze or clay lamps filled with olive oil or cooking grease for night use. In only the very finest inns will guests find candles

because the many churches throughout the city hold a monopoly on them.

Before going to bed, guests may take a bath in a large basin and use a latrine that empties down a tile drain spout to the underground system of sewers. Guests to the city will appreciate the modern sewage system consisting of a complex network of lead pipes beneath the entire city that carries wastewater to the sea.

Some inns provide meals for their customers willing to pay higher rates. Bear in mind, however, that city laws prevent innkeepers from serving breakfast before 8:00 A.M. on days of festivals and Sundays, and after 8:00 P.M. when the city orders all fires extinguished (except for those needed by bakers to prepare the next morning's breads).

Finding a Bite to Eat

Constantinople can provide a plethora of different places to find a bite to eat. Many different types of restaurants abound throughout the city, advertising with a sign like this: εστιατόριο. If you wish to sit down for a meal, many restaurants in the low-number districts along the east end of the city serve grilled meats, lamb chops, and spiced ground lamb. Most restaurant owners will invite foreign-speaking patrons who have not mastered Greek into their kitchen to see the dishes. If anyone does not believe the delicacies that can be found here, consider this letter sent from a Roman emissary back to friends in Rome describing Constantinople's fare:

A City Awash in Freshwater

Constantinople is awash in crystal clear water. Today's visitors will find the city modern and clean in every way. No city can boast a larger or healthier supply of freshwater than Constantinople, which channels water through aqueducts from artesian wells and lakes throughout the surrounding hillsides. Eight of these aqueducts dump tens of millions of gallons daily into the city, either to dispersion points such as fountains or into a system of covered, underground cisterns. All of this is at no cost to the citizenry.

From the eight initial dispersal locations, pipes beneath the streets carry water to secondary distribution points where families, restaurateurs, and innkeepers draw their daily water. Other locations provide for watering animals. There are even a few privately owned pipes that carry water directly to the villas of the rich and powerful. The many public and private baths scattered throughout the city also consume huge daily volumes of water.

In addition to immediate distribution of freshwater, some is diverted to the many underground cisterns for storage in the event of drought or attack against the city. The largest of them, the Basilica Cistern built by Emperor Justinian, covers an area of approximately 100,000 square feet. Within this cavernous underground grotto, 336 marble columns 40 feet tall prevent the roof from collapsing. The total volume, 4 million cubic feet, contains 30 million gallons when full.

Constantinople pipes freshwater from the hills to huge cisterns where it is stored against drought or attack.

I ordered him [the waiter] to send to me from among his most delicate dishes a fat goat, deliciously stuffed with garlic, onions and leeks; steeped in fish sauce: a dish which I could have wished just then to be upon your table, so that you who do not believe the delicacies of Constantinople to be desirable, should at length become believers at this sight![10]

Besides garlic goat, other favorite main dishes include roast pork basted in honey and wine, lamb or beef wrapped in a crusty pastry shell, a variety of baked fish caught in the local waters, and several fowl dishes. Many types of chewy rice and wheat hors d'oeuvre are served with the main dish, as is a biscuit called *paximadion* that is often made from barley and then covered in butter, olive oil, or honey. Tourists will notice that bread is so important to everyone's meal that each baker stamps his bread with a logo identifying his product. Desserts range from honey dripped over fresh fruits to a sweet variation of *paximadion* made from butter-based dough that comes in a variety of

Honey, olives, grain, and game are a few of the foods available in restaurants and from street vendors.

spice flavors such as aniseed, vanilla, cinnamon, and occasionally mint. Expect to pay between one and one and a half *seliquas* for such a meal.

Finer restaurants in Constantinople, such as the one the Roman emissary chose, are particular about not only the look of their fare but the quality as well. "Fresh meat" means that it was slaughtered and delivered that morning, which is why visitors will see delivery men carrying skinned goats and lambs slung over their shoulders and around their necks as they negotiate the city's narrow streets. When the quality of the meat is poor, restaurateurs will complain to their provider of animals. One restaurant owner is reported to have reprimanded his supplier by stating, "Above all, provide a good pig for the occasion, but see that it *is* a good one, not a lean useless thing like the last time."[11]

Often more fun than eating in restaurants, however, is eating on the go. Newcomers strolling along the larger streets will see many food vendors wandering right along with them. Vendors of milk, vegetables, fruits, juices, and meat wrapped in bread trace a path up and down the streets, often calling out the names of the goods they carry. Tourists will enjoy the unusual sight of seeing locals purchasing food by calling out to the vendor from the upper-story windows of their homes and shops. Following a moment of haggling over the prices, the local will lower a bucket or an old sheet with the money for the vendor, who will then fill the bucket or sheet with the purchased goods.

If keeping up with jostling vendors seems too unnerving, you may want to find something to eat in the numerous commercial markets that advertise their locations with unbelievably wonderful smells. You will be dazzled by the amazing variety of delicacies that can be found in such markets. Most of the foods are sold directly from pushcarts stationed along the sides of the streets. Common sorts of foods that are carted fresh into the city every morning include: a variety of cheeses, cut pieces of roasted pork wrapped in a wheat bread, bread dipped in honey or olive oil, eggs, fresh yogurts, roasted turbot, giant shrimps, olives, whole honeycombs, a variety of herbs, and local wines. There will also be colorful vegetables from the countryside including beets, cabbage, lettuce, carrots, onions, and radishes.

Visitors who buy their lunches from pushcart owners can rest assured that they have not been cheated by disreputable owners because city officials set the prices for foods sold there. Inspectors also make regular visits to the markets to be certain that the prices are not increased.

Once visitors have a feel for the activities of the city, they can freely plan their stay and take advantage of the city's unique offerings. For those planning a short stay, the first activity recommended is a day visiting Constantinople's three great architectural treasures: the Church of Hagia Sophia, the Imperial Palace, and the Hippodrome. Fortunately, one full day will be sufficient because all three are grouped close together at the eastern tip of the city.

CHAPTER FOUR

Architectural Treasures

When Constantine ordained Constantinople the new capital of the Roman Empire in 330, he intended the city to look like the capital of a great empire. One of the ingredients in the making of a great city is its monumental architecture. Just as Athens, Jerusalem, Cairo, and Rome act as magnets for travelers because of their famed buildings and monuments, so too does Constantinople. Three structures in particular that bring pride to all Constantinopolitans are the Church of Hagia Sophia, the Imperial Palace, and the Hippodrome. Fortunately for tourists, they are located in districts two, three, and four, and a visit to all three can be accomplished in a one-day tour. Start with Hagia Sophia, located in district two atop the Acropolis. To find it, simply follow the signs reading ίαγία σοφία.

Hagia Sophia

The church Hagia Sophia, meaning divine wisdom, was built by Emperor Constantine to be the city's crowning Christian church. Unfortunately, it was completely destroyed by fire during a riot in 532. The church standing before you today is the replacement designed by the architects Anthemius of Tralles and Isidore of Miletus and dedicated by Emperor Justinian in 537. The great dome, however, collapsed in 558 due to an earthquake; the dome you see today immediately took its place. One of the most poetic descriptions of the church comes from a man who knew it well, the historian Procopius who witnessed the dedication by Justinian:

The Church presents a most glorious spectacle, extraordinary to those who behold it and altogether incredible to those who are told of it. In height it rises to the very heavens and overtops the neighboring houses like a ship anchored among them, appearing above a city it adorns and forms a part of. . . . It is distinguished by indescribable beauty, excelling both in its size and in the harmony of its measures.[12]

Before entering this great cathedral, take a few minutes to walk the perimeter gardens to get a feel for its massive size—64,000 square feet—and how it curves to form its main dome as well as several smaller ones. The church is nearly square—measuring 250 by 256 feet—and the impressive dome soars 201 feet and arches 107 feet across, the largest in the world. The reddish hue given to the exterior stucco imparts a warmth that glows in the morning and evening sun and is one of the reasons it is considered the most important landmark for mariners approaching the city.

Entry is through the massive bronze front doors. First-time visitors are known to nearly fall backwards as they crane their heads to take in the full view of the cavernous interior bathed in light from the forty arched windows that surround the dome and dozens more on the side walls.

Compared to the church's exterior, the interior is a dazzling jewelry box. The finest and rarest materials from the four corners of the empire were brought to

Emperor Constantine built Hagia Sophia to be Constantinople's crowning Christian church.

Constantinople to adorn this masterpiece. The porphyry marble columns, reddish in color, were previously taken to Rome from an Egyptian temple in Heliopolis, and from Rome they found their way here. The polychrome marble on the walls and floors, primarily white with green highlights, came from throughout Greece and Italy, and the inlays of ivory, pearls, and gold icons came from ancient temples in Ephesus.

The nave, the center section where parishioners sit, is 120 feet wide and the two aisles on either side add an additional 58 feet each, creating a total interior width of 236 feet running along the

Procopius on Hagia Sophia

The only description of Hagia Sophia at the time Emperor Justinian rebuilt the church in 537 was provided by the historian Procopius who attended the dedication. His description of the church, recorded in his book, De Aedificiis, *is the only document describing the vast interior of what he called the Great Church:*

The Great Church is distinguished by indescribable beauty, excelling both in its size, and in the harmony of its measures, having no part excessive and none deficient; being more magnificent than ordinary buildings, and much more elegant than those which are not of so just a proportion. The church is singularly full of light and sunshine; you would declare that the place is not lighted by the sun from without, but that the rays are produced within itself, such an abundance of light is poured into this church.

Now above the arches is raised a circular building of a curved form through which the light of day first shines; for the building, which I imagine overtops the whole country, has small openings left on purpose, so that the places where these intervals occur may serve for the light to come through. Thus far I imagine the building is not incapable of being described, even by a weak and feeble tongue. As the arches are arranged in a quadrangular figure, the stone-work between them takes the shape of a triangle; the lower angle of each triangle, being compressed where the arches unite, is slender, while the upper part becomes wider as it rises in the space between them, and ends against the circle which rests upon them, forming there its remaining angles. A spherical-shaped dome standing upon this circle makes it exceedingly beautiful; from the lightness of the building, it does not appear to rest upon a solid foundation, but to cover the place beneath as though it were suspended from heaven by the fabled golden chain. All these parts surprisingly joined to one another in the air, suspended one from another, and resting only on that which is next to them, form the work into one admirably harmonious whole, which spectators do not dwell upon for long in the mass, as each individual part attracts the eye to itself.

A cross section of Hagia Sophia reveals the architectural intricacy and beauty of the church's interior.

north-south axis. Look around the vast interior and you will see the four massive concrete piers, each 100 square feet, supporting the enormous weight of the dome. By placing these four piers at the four corners of the church, the bearing structure is largely hidden from the eye, creating the impression that space expands in all directions and that the dome floats in the air. For lightness, grace, and proportion, the effect is unrivaled.

While wandering throughout the spacious interior, take some time to view the many mosaics, depicting both religious and secular scenes, set along the walls.

One of the more interesting of historical interest can be found in the lunette, or small window, over the south doorway. This image is of Justinian presenting a model of Hagia Sophia to the Virgin Mary and the Christ child. Besides this well-known mosaic, dozens of others depict biblical scenes from the New Testament, as well as previous emperors and their families.

The next architectural masterpiece on today's tour is the Imperial Palace. Getting there from Hagia Sophia is a snap because it is close by. So close, in fact, that Justinian and his successors had direct access to both by a bridge crossing over Augustaeum

The Beauty of Mosaics

Some of the true treasures of Constantinople are the hundreds of mosaics found in the dozens of churches throughout the city. Fashioned from tiny bits of glass, ceramic tile, stone, and occasionally gems, mosaics are one artistic medium most guests to the city associate with Constantinople. Beautiful examples of this wondrous art form can be found in private homes, shops, and the Imperial Palace, but the best place to experience their dramatic colors and designs is in the churches.

Mosaics are unique creations that tell stories. Unlike the stories told by the fluid application of paint, mosaics tell their stories with thousands, and sometimes tens of thousands, of colorful cubes called tesserae, often no larger than one quarter of an inch. The creators of mosaics approach a work much like a painter does: deciding upon a theme, location, layout, colors, and style. The tesserae are then set closely to-

Halos and robe colors identify the central figures in religious mosaics to the illiterate.

gether in a thin base of cement to hold them permanently in place. When completed and viewed from a distance of twenty feet or more, the works appear to be painted.

The mosaics enjoyed throughout our churches typically tell biblical stories that can be easily and quickly recognized and understood. The stories most commonly told in tesserae are important events in the life of Christ such as his birth, baptism, teachings, death on the cross, and resurrection. To the common people, most of whom are illiterate, identifying the major figures in the Bible is important. For this reason, mosaicists typically depict Christ with a gold halo; long, light-colored hair and beard; and wearing gold or purple robes. St. Peter always has a rounded, white beard and is wearing brown robes; St. Paul is always bald and wearing gray clothes.

Square that separates the two sites. When exiting the church, head straight across the square (under the bridge). Proceed to the main entry gate called the Chalkê or Brazen Gate because its doors are made of burnished bronze. Do not arrive later than one in the afternoon because the gates are promptly closed to the public at three.

The Imperial Palace

The Chalkê Gate sets the tone for the Imperial Palace. Connected to the great doors is a covered entry area lavishly decorated with mosaics depicting military triumphs of Justinian's great general Belisarius, and the walkway is made of exquisite polychrome marble—mostly reds, greens, whites, and blues.

Passing through the gate, visitors feel the full extent of the Imperial Palace that was built by Constantine and enlarged by Justinian and several of their successors. The palace, far from being a single structure housing the royal family, is now a complex of residences and municipal buildings needed to house all of the government officials that command the Eastern Roman Empire. Although most buildings are closed to the public, visitors are welcome to stroll through the ornately sculptured gardens while viewing the exteriors of the palace buildings in grounds made beautiful with fountains and trees. The views are commanding across the Sea of Marmara and east to the hills and mountains on the Asiatic side of the Bosphorus.

A stroll toward the south leads visitors down elegantly planted paths dotted with water fountains that cascade over six different terrace levels on the slope between the Hippodrome and the sea. Walking along this path takes visitors past the indoor family riding school, a great grassy expanse where polo is played; a long reflecting pool; and a smattering of buildings housing staff, horses, and storerooms.

This path is the same one used by the royal family and their guests when descending to Bukoleon Harbor, where royal yachts tie up awaiting family excursions across the water. Here too visitors will find Bukoleon Palace, the main living quarters for the royal family while staying within the walls of the Imperial Palace. Bukoleon Palace is built down to the sea on top of the seawalls that were widened to support the additional weight.

While at the small imperial harbor, take a few moments to inspect the lighthouse, the largest in the world. Made entirely of stone, the lighthouse's topmost part, where the fire is maintained, is lined with bronze to contain the heat and to reflect the light as far out to sea as possible. The small house next to it is the permanent home for the fire crew who tend the fire all night long.

Security for the royal family and members of the government requires that they have their own small, private, underground aqueduct and cistern located near the northwest corner of the grounds. One

Mosaics set in the pathways of the Imperial Palace show everyday street scenes from the time of Constantine to the present.

of the pleasures of taking the walk in that direction is the beautifully designed and crafted mosaics set in the path across the top of the palace grounds. The pathway presents a pictorial history of the royal family, as well as everyday street scenes of Constantinople since the time of Constantine. A slow pace allows sightseers to recognize scenes depicting the marketplaces, donkeys bearing goods into the city under the watchful eyes of the owners' slaves, horse races, wild animals found only in far-away places (such as lions, hippopotamuses, and rhinoceroses from Egypt), as well as children playing in the streets.

Leaving the Imperial Palace means departing the way you came, through the Chalkê Gate. While wandering in that direction, take a moment to admire the many different types and colors of marble imported to cover the exterior of the buildings within this compound. Once out the gate, make a left turn past a small domed structure, the Milion Arch, the spot where the official distances to all major cities within the empire are inscribed.

At this point, you might hear a thunderous sound coming from the crowds just around the corner at the last stop on today's tour, the Hippodrome, where chariot racing takes place most days of the week. This is a good time to stop for a quick bite to eat from one of the dozens of pushcart vendors selling grilled chunks of lamb smothered in a sauce of cucumber and yogurt. Wash it down with a cup of fruit juice from another vendor, and you will be ready to go again until dinner. In the event that the Hippodrome is closed and quiet for the day, a sign reading ἱππoςδρόμος will at least confirm you have arrived at the correct site.

The Hippodrome

Second to none, the Hippodrome is the favorite entertainment place for Constantinopolitan men. This great edifice, more than any other in the city, is indisputably the place of the common man. Gargantuan in scale, this gleaming white marble monolith, shaped like an elongated horseshoe (rounded at one end but square at the other), is the largest structure in the city—1560 feet long and 380 feet wide. From within the stadium, the towering dome of Hagia Sophia is a visible backdrop for everyone. Begun in A.D. 198 by Emperor Septimius Severus, it later grew to its present size as part of Emperor Constantine's building program to recreate some of the architectural grandeur of Rome.

Capable of holding sixty thousand spectators, the Hippodrome is principally used for chariot races, but it also functions as the largest venue in the city for many other spectacles. Occasionally, other events take place there such as footraces, boxing, sideshows of deformed people and animals, or wild animal hunts (where animals prey on each other or hunters kill the animals with spears or bows and arrows). Public executions and sometimes fights to the death between enemy soldiers captured in wars also take place here for those of hardier constitution. The world traveler Benjamin of Tudela recently witnessed an annual Christmas event:

Roman emperor Septimius Severus began building the Hippodrome.

Close to the walls of the palace is also a place of amusement belonging to the emperor, which is called the Hippodrome, and every year on the anniversary of the birth of Jesus the emperor gives a great entertainment there. And in that place men from all the races of the world come with jugglery and without jugglery, and they introduce lions, leopards, bears, and wild asses, and they engage them in combat with one another; and the same thing is done with birds. No entertainment like this is to be found in any other land.[13]

If seats are available, enter and proceed to the arena seating area. The cost of entry is always a pleasant surprise—no cost at all—because the races are subsidized by the state and private citizens. Gazing down at the chariot track, visitors will see the *spina*, the spine or backbone, consisting of a low, thin wall extending the length of the track except for the two turns at each end. This wall prohibits chariots charging down one side from colliding with chariots coming down the other. Situated on the low wall are two large decorative columns, both about thirty feet tall. One is an obelisk honoring Constantine; it was brought here

Capable of accomodating sixty thousand spectators, the Hippodrome is used for entertainment, executions, and chariot races.

from the Temple of Karnak in Egypt. The other column, brought from Delphi in Greece, honors the Greek warriors who fought against the Persians at the Battle of Marathon during the fifth century B.C.

Moving sixty thousand people in and out of the Hippodrome in an orderly manner required an efficient design for the stadium. To accomplish such a task, entry on the street level is aided by numbered arched openings extending all the way around the perimeter. Once inside, whether on the first or second level, people can easily find their seats with the help of well-positioned staircases. The efficiency of the seating process includes a metal token given to each spectator that has stamped on it the number of the arched entry, first or second level, and the section and seat number.

There is also a place where spectators, in the midst of chariot races or animal hunts, can voice their dissatisfaction to the emperor if he is present. The emperor, not intimidated by the verbal jousts, readily replies from his royal box.

The emperor is quite willing to engage in verbal taunting, but not outright disloyalty. Once, the Hippodrome was the site of a grisly incident. In January 532, when Justinian was emperor, the most horrific event in the history of the Hippodrome occurred following weeks of rioting by citizens who sought to seize control of the city and government from Justinian. The rioters ran to the Hippodrome to listen to speeches and to plan their rebellion against the emperor. During this dark moment for the city, the soldiers remained loyal and encircled the jam-packed stadium. Then, at an order, they entered the Hippodrome, trapping and slaughtering an estimated thirty thousand dissidents. No such tragedy has occurred since then, and visitors will be overcome by the splendor of the arena so as not to dwell on dark events.

A strenuous full day in the sun walking through the city's finest monumental architecture deserves a few days of casual sightseeing. The most beautiful, culturally enriching, and historically interesting sightseeing trips will take visitors through the city on boats, wagons, and by foot. Taking in all of them will require at least three days because they are spread throughout the city and because the most popular, the boat ride along the Bosphorus, is a whole day's activity in itself.

CHAPTER FIVE

Casual Sightseeing

A stay in Constantinople is not complete without the traditional and unforgettable excursion by boat on the Bosphorus. Along its shores is a surprising mixture of past and present, grand splendor and simple beauty. The shore is lined with modern inns, palaces of marble, old fortresses, and small fishing villages.

Excursion boats that regularly zigzag along the Bosphorus shores depart from Phosphorion Harbor on the Golden Horn in district four. At the harbor you will see every imaginable kind and size of vessel, from small fishing boats that tie up and sell their freshly caught fish, to three-hundred-oar warships called *dromons*. The round trip excursion takes the entire day, and the fare is reasonably priced at one *seliqua* (price includes lunch). The excursion boats, which are rowed to guarantee a timely return to the harbor at the end of the day, stop alternately on the Asian and European sides.

The first stop on the Asian side, at the city of Chalcedon, is a visit to the city's Acropolis, the tallest hill on either side of the Bosphorus. From the top of the Acropolis, tourists can gaze back and admire the magnificent panorama of Constantinople across the straits. From this vantage point, the districts along the point of Constantinople's peninsula and the city's famous monumental architecture can be most appreciated. Looking down at the city, everyone will be able to pick out Hagia Sophia, the Imperial Palace and its magnificent gardens, the lighthouse, the Hippodrome, and the Forum of Constantine—they seem close enough to touch. Before heading down the hill, take a moment to appreciate the strategic significance of the Golden Horn Estuary, and wonder how the first settlers here, more than sixteen hundred years ago, missed the opportunity to settle across the straits.

The boat will travel most of the twenty miles toward the Black Sea, passing

Women's Appearance on the Street

Although they will not be seen in large numbers, women of Constantinople enjoy getting out into the streets just as much as the men. The hustle of the streets is largely the domain of male merchants, but women are also seen scurrying from place to place to purchase household necessities. There are numerous other reasons for excursions outside the home: to visit the public baths; to go to church services; to visit religious relics; to see a holy man; to attend religious processions and funerals; or to attend family celebrations, such as the birth of a child or a wedding. It is, however, considered unseemly for a woman to attend chariot races or other bloody spectacles at the Hippodrome.

The prevalent ideal of modesty for women demands that when they appear in public they wear garments that conceal virtually all of their body except for their hands and faces. Typical garb is a full-length, long-sleeved tunic, with additional layers added as necessary for warmth. Lower-class women might wear sleeveless tunics. Proper women are always seen with their heads covered when they are out in public; they wear the *maphorion*, a long veil over a tight headdress that conceals their hair but not their faces.

Women of means devote much to their personal appearance, spending large sums of money on woven fabrics, sometimes embroidered and encrusted with precious stones. They further adorn their garments with brooches and jeweled sashes or belts, and wear elegant *maphorions*. They decorate their hair with hairpins and ornamented mesh nets and bands. The examples of jewelry foreign travelers will see include earrings, bracelets, and necklaces that demonstrate the fine workmanship of Byzantine goldsmiths and the wealth of the upper classes. Less wealthy women also enjoy jewelry, but cannot afford real gems and must settle for imitations.

Paste gems decorate jewelry for those of modest means.

Much to the dismay of the church fathers and some husbands, travelers today may see some women who enhance their natural beauty with cosmetics. Commonly used techniques include: powdering their faces with bean or wheat flour to make their complexions fairer; applying an assortment of colored clay substances to redden their lips and cheeks or to darken their eyebrows and eye lashes; and dying their hair different colors.

small fishing villages and stopping at one for a fish lunch and fruit drinks. On the way, the excursion boat will dodge larger freighters from Russia carrying their cargoes of lumber for new buildings, furs for elegant winter coats and boots, honey, and wax. Occasionaly, a shipload of slaves chained to the decks will pass by on their way to be sold in the city's slave market.

Following a day on an excursion boat, the other recommended sites to be seen can be reached on foot, by horse, or by rented litters carried on the shoulders of four men. There are three significant collections of holy relics for Christians to see, beginning with the best at the Imperial Palace.

Visiting Holy Relics

Constantinopolitans are fiercely proud of their Christian faith. As the largest Christian city in the world and having the largest church in the world, Constantinopole boasts local Christians who are staunch defenders of their traditions. Much of the Christian fervor stems from the city's close proximity to the Holy Land where Jesus was born, taught his message of tolerance and forgiveness, died on the cross, and was then resurrected. Because of this proximity, Constantinople has accumulated the largest collection of holy relics and artifacts from the time of Jesus of any city. Thousands of Christians from Europe visit our city each year on their pilgrimage to the Holy Land, stopping here to be emotionally moved by the city's collection, and in so doing, some seek miracle cures for their illnesses from the power of the holy relics.

The most significant collection of relics is kept carefully guarded in the Imperial Palace. Pilgrims wishing to see this collection need to obtain permission from either the royal family or the patriarch of Constantinople, the city's chief religious leader. This collection is said to contain the holiest relics found anywhere. At the center of the collection is the holy cross found by Saint Helena who then gave it to her son, Emperor Constantine, at the beginning of the fourth century. Ever since then, emperors have tried to expand the collection that now also includes the crown of thorns, the holy spear that pierced Jesus' side while nailed to the cross, and Jesus' funeral linens.

Another collection worth examining happens to be right across the street at Hagia Sophia. Since it is conveniently found nearby, wander over and have a look at its remarkable collection of treasures.

The most important relics found here are not related directly to Christ but are of inestimable value nonetheless. The church has nine very old gospel books, two of which are still used by the priests; the other seven, adorned in gold and silver, are kept in the *skeuophylakion*, the church treasury. Also carefully guarded there are five baptismal bowls, fourteen jewel encrusted chalices, six sacred *lavides* (spoons), six silver patriarchal staffs, four candelabra by the church's entrance, eight crosses containing splinters of the true cross (and adorned with gold, silver,

A gold reliquary, in the form of a Byzantine cross, is said to contain a piece of the true cross.

and pearls), a few icons, hieratic vestments, and a scattering of some relics belonging to various saints.

After admiring the Hagia Sophia collection, the next stop should be to visit the second most impressive collection of relics after those kept in the Imperial Palace. This collection resides in the Church of the Holy Apostles on the hill northwest of the Aqueduct of Valens. Upon exiting Hagia Sophia, turn right and walk west down Mesê Street ten blocks.

The Church of the Holy Apostles was erected in 330 by Emperor Constantine,

who built within the church a large cross-shaped tomb intended for his own burial. He also prepared twelve empty caskets that were to receive the remains of the Twelve Apostles. In 356, the Emperor Constantius brought and deposited under the altar the skulls of three apostles: Andrew from Achaia, Luke the Evangelist, and Timothy from Ephesus. In addition to seeking out these sacred skulls, pilgrims visiting here should also remember to find the column of flagellation, the wood column to which Jesus was once bound in order to be flogged.

Next on the tour is a visit to the city's famous, easy-to-find land wall. Standing just three miles west of the Imperial Palace, it is easily reached by taking Mesê Street all the way to the Gate of Charisius, which is part of the wall.

A Visit to the City's Land Wall

The elaborate defense walls surrounding Constantinople make it the best-fortified city in the world. This enormous wall, dwarfing any that surround European cities, is one of the most fascinating and complex examples of utilitarian architecture and is well worth a visit.

The land wall stretches on a north-south axis across the three-and-a-half-mile neck of land between the Golden Horn Estuary to the north and the Sea of Marmara to the south. The wall defines the most western extent of the city. It is the only stretch of wall that does not conform to the coastline, hence it is referred

The elaborate system of walls defending Constantinople makes the city the most fortified in the world.

to as the land wall to distinguish it from the many seawalls.

The best way to tour the land wall is to exit the city and walk a mile in either direction to appreciate its size and complexity. One of the first observations that visitors will make is that the wall is actually a defensive system composed of three separate walls, placed one behind the other, and fronted by a moat. This design maximizes the difficulty that enemies experience when trying to invade the city.

The moat is the first obstacle. Today it is empty, but it can be quickly flooded (with water brought in through pipes from the Golden Horn) to a depth of 22 feet and a width of 60 feet. If invaders manage to ford the moat, they will then encounter a 61-foot-wide embankment that leads up to the outer wall. This wall, the first of the three stone walls, is 20 feet tall and shields the first bank of archers. Behind the first wall is the second wall, 7 feet thick at the base and 3 feet thick at the

Visiting the Universities

The largest city in the European and Asian continents is also the best educated. Many wealthy families from other lands send their sons here to gain their educations before returning home to practice law, medicine, theology, or business. While visiting, many educated travelers might wish to take advantage of the opportunity to see firsthand some of the city's famed schools and meet with their faculties. As one scholar points out in the book *Byzantine Civilization*, "Foreign travelers are deeply impressed by the range of education and the purity of the Greek spoken by the inhabitants of the city."

Universities range from very small private academies owned by the faculty and catering to one to five students, to larger, more well-known institutions—such as St. Peter's or the University of Lakapenos—that have as many as one hundred students enrolled. In addition to many lay universities, several churches also serve as advanced-learning centers. These universities, which have an actual meeting place for study and libraries for research, are far more advanced than any in Europe that lack such amenities. Although these universities are small, visitors interested in visiting any of them will find the faculty knowledgeable and courses of study rigorous.

Perhaps the single most salient aspect of Byzantine culture is the transmission of classical culture. While classical studies, science, law, medicine, and philosophy are largely lacking in Europe at this time, Constantinople universities still zealously pursue these intellectual traditions. It is in Constantinople that Plato and Aristotle continue to be studied and here that they are translated from Greek into many languages. And a basic education in Constantinople consists first of the mastery of classical Greek literature, such as Homer, Plato, and Aristotle.

Students in Constantinople use wax tablets like this one to help master their classical curriculum.

The relationship between teachers and students goes far beyond classroom education. Parents expect their sons to be cared for while away from home, and many letters between teachers and parents address classroom discipline, dormitories, food, moral character, and the need for tuition money. Classrooms are always open to the public, so feel free to wander in and join recitations—in Greek—of some of the greatest ancient thinkers. Be certain that your accent is good because few things will irritate a teacher more than a poor fifth-century Greek accent!

top, where archers can shoot down at the enemy 30 feet below. Adding greater defensive complexity to this second wall are 92 watchtowers rising 35 feet. Finally, the third and largest of the walls, 14 feet thick and standing 60 feet tall, bristles with 96 watchtowers, 70 feet tall and spaced 60 yards apart. Of the 96 watchtowers, six serve the dual purpose of acting as city gates that can be opened and closed.

Each of the watchtowers is built into the wall and extends fifteen feet out from it. This design serves two principal purposes: First, it allows defenders to see the other towers and to communicate with them by coded signals. Second, the watchtowers provide defenders an elevated place where they can shoot arrows, drop heavy stones, throw down burning twigs, or pour boiling oil and water on attackers attempting to scale the walls.

During sustained periods of peace, such as Constantinople now experiences, only a skeleton guard occupies these formidable defenses. Years of successful defense of the city, however, have proven the wall impregnable when the city's full complement of soldiers is on guard.

If these massive walls fire your imagination, head back into the city and visit the Aqueduct of Valens that parallels Mesê Street. Stop almost anywhere along the way to inspect and discover the second of the city's most remarkable examples of massive utilitarian architecture.

The Aqueduct of Valens

The massive two-story limestone aqueduct off to your left as you wander down Mesê Street is the Aqueduct of Valens, the oldest, largest, and most impressive of the city's eight aqueducts. This is a monument to clean water that runs all the way down to the Imperial Palace.

Begun in 343 and completed thirty years later by the Emperor Valens, the aqueduct begins ninety-three miles west of the city. The double-tiered arches, seventy-three feet above the ground, support a channel that carries water from nearby lakes along the very top. Only those visitors adventuresome enough to climb to the top will actually see the water. Although it is not recommended, the structure can be climbed, and anyone who does so will discover that the trough at the top is covered with heavy stone tiles that keep the water clean. Beneath the tiles, which are removable to provide access, is the three-by-five-foot trough that daily transports several million gallons to the city.

The structure of the Valens aqueduct is truly impressive. One of the most remarkable facts about the aqueduct is that the millions of limestone blocks were set together without the use of concrete. The masons cut and placed the stones so precisely that they have withstood the wear and tear of more than six hundred years. The stones are rigidly held in place by their sheer weight and the weight of the water carried along the top. The arches are superbly designed to support the total weight: They transfer the tremendous pressures to their sides and down the massive piers to the ground.

Find your way back to Mesê Street and continue east until the large, circular forum built by and named after the Emperor Constantine comes into view. Of the many forums in Constantinople, this one is the largest, most decorated, and most noteworthy.

The Forum of Constantine

The Forum of Constantine occupies a strategic place in Constantinople's downtown congestion, but its purpose to sight-seers is not so obvious. When Emperor Constantine began construction on this central gathering place, with its distinctive oval shape surrounded by colonnades and two monumental gates set in the east and west ends, the populace thought it would function as a commercial center and nothing more. But as construction continued, the people realized that besides being used as a place where merchants and buyers could transact business, it would also be used as an important center for government.

On the north side of the forum, Constantine built the Senate House that

Precise stonecutting and block placement eliminate the need for concrete in the Valens aqueduct, the oldest of the city's eight aqueducts.

stands there today. Unlike the very simple Senate House in Rome, this one has a large, impressive entry porch with four big columns and a circular meeting area with a domed roof called a rotunda.

Next Constantine added the mammoth 185-foot red granite column, named the Porphyry Column or Burnt Column because of its color, to the center of the forum. This column is so large that those taking a close look at it will notice that it is not one single piece of marble but rather eight column drums stacked one on top of another. Constantine disassembled the column and brought it here from the Temple of Apollo in Rome. He then removed the statue of Apollo from the top, replacing it with the statue seen today. It is a likeness of Constantine himself, wearing a sun-crown (with rays radiating from the center) on his head, and holding a scepter in one hand and a globe in the other. Completing the theme of the sun, a bronze statue depicting a four-horse chariot, called a *quadriga*, driven by Constantine as *Sol Invictus*, the Invincible Sun, is brought here from the Hippodrome each year on May 11 in a grand procession. The procession commemorates the beginning of the senatorial session for the year.

The Forum of Constantine is just one of several forums where the buying and selling of merchandise takes place. In addition to them, the entire length of Mesê Street is a marketplace as are dozens of other side streets with tiny shops where merchants sell their goods. The many marketplaces make for the best shopping experiences possible since the decline of Rome, Alexandria, and Athens. For visitors who still have a few *solidi* in their coin bags, Constantinople is the best place to find rare and elegant souvenirs to take home.

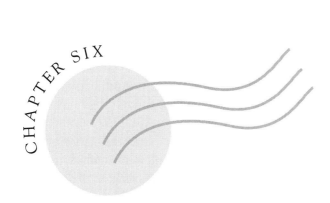

CHAPTER SIX

Shopping

Constantinople is the marketplace to the world. No city in Europe or Asia can boast a greater variety of goods or items of better quality. Shopping is one of the highlights of a visit to this city. Travelers who regularly voyage from as far away as England, Egypt, Russia, Persia, and India all agree that Constantinople is the city of choice to purchase the most amazing and exotic products they have seen. Benjamin of Tudela certainly thought so while visiting our luxurious city when he said of the finely clad Constantinopolitans:

> The Greek inhabitants are very rich in gold and precious stones, and they go clothed in garments of silk with gold embroidery, and they ride horses, and look like princes. Indeed, the land is very rich in all cloth stuffs, and in bread, meat, and wine. Wealth like that of Constantinople is not to be found in the whole world.[14]

Constantinople is particularly enchanting for European travelers because within its city walls are warehouses filled with exotic goods from mystical Asia but very little from Western Europe. As a rule, the economic and cultural depression that has paralyzed Europe since the collapse of the Roman Empire several hundred years ago has rendered it a manufacturing wasteland compared with the goods being manufactured in Asia and shipped for sale to Constantinople.

Finding the best shopping opportunities is thrilling and easy—just wander down Mesê Street. This main commercial artery features row after row of merchants' stalls that line both sides of the street. Placed here to attract customers, the temporary stalls (that go up in the day and down at night) are shaded by enormous, colorful canopies that snap in the breeze while tethered to wooded posts.

Nearest the Imperial Palace, in district number one, are the perfumers and spice merchants. Farther up Mesê Street are silversmiths and money changers and, at the Forum of Constantine in district six, is the center of the fur trade. Near the Hippodrome, in district three, stands the House of Lamps, so called not because it sells lamps but because its windows are lamp-lit at night to show off the finest dyed silks available.

Everything imaginable for sale can be found in Constantinople, but most travelers come here to take home goods not usually found in their cities. The most unusual merchandise available here but not in many other cities includes silk fabrics, carpets, illuminated manuscripts, spices, and clothing.

Silk

Constantinople and beautiful silk fabrics are talked about as though they have belonged together forever. Do not miss this opportunity to explore the city's enormous collection. Laws regulating the manufacture and sale of silk include a ban on exportation, and for this reason, thousands flock here annually just for the experience of buying our world-renowned silk dresses, shoes, and brocades.

Dress shops offer shoppers the largest selection of silk products outside of China. For hundreds of years the secrets of silk production and manufacture had been a closely guarded and vigorously defended secret. Before about 550, all silk

The Emperor Justinian accepts a bamboo cane containing eggs of the silkworm, the beginning of Constantinople's silk industry.

Raising Silkworms

The unique physical properties of silk, which include fineness, strength, and ability to absorb rich colors, are the result of the cocoons spun by silkworms. The price buyers pay for this fabric is indeed high, but the process, the time required, and the uniqueness of the material justifies the high cost.

Tiny cocoons are unraveled and spun together to make silk thread.

The silk process starts with tiny silkworm eggs laid by a queen. The eggs are so small that each is barely visible: One ounce contains about twenty thousand. Following three months of storage in a cool place, the tiny eggs hatch into a mass of worms that are less than one-half inch long. The worms quickly acquire a voracious appetite, consuming enormous volumes of mulberry leaves, their main food source. During their lifetime, the twenty thousand will eat a ton of mulberry leaves. While maturing, the worms spin their silk cocoons in preparation for becoming silk moths. During this stage of development, which takes three months, the worms have increased their weight ten thousand times from the day they hatched from their eggs.

The cocoon is the final stage of development from the point of view of the silkworm farmers. Each cocoon is a single exceptionally fine silk filament about two thousand feet long. Before the worms can fully develop into moths and break from their cocoons, they are collected and placed in hot water. This kills the worms and loosens the cocoon filaments. If the moths were allowed to break from their cocoons, as they do in the wild, much of the silk would be destroyed. Ten to twelve of the harvested filaments are then spun together to form a single thread.

Once the silk threads are wound on spools, each spool is dipped in a dye that will permanently color the thread. One of the qualities of silk is its ability to fully absorb the dye without diminishing the color (as is the case with cotton and wool). After a thorough drying process, the threads are woven into the intricate designs that are sold in the many silk markets throughout cities such as Constantinople. The cost is understandable considering that after one year one thousand cocoons have produced 2 million feet of filament—which will create only four ounces of finished silk material.

clothing in Constantinople came from China. Then, two monks appeared before Emperor Justinian with silkworm eggs hidden in their hollow bamboo walking canes. Under the monks' supervision the eggs hatched into worms, the worms spun cocoons, and the silk merchants of Constantinople were at last in the silk business.

Silk can be found everywhere that wanderers of the city's streets choose to go. Clothes are the most obvious use for silk material but by no means the only one. For generations, silk banners of every imaginable color have hung from buildings serving as billowing announcements for festivals and other civic events. Sailors covet silk for its remarkable strength that makes superior ropes and even silk sails that power small sailing ships through the Bosphorus.

For shoppers, however, Constantinople and silk are associated with elegant clothing and shoes that can be found at several locations throughout the city. Odo of Deuil, the abbot of St. Denis, remarked on Contantinopolitans and their unique attire: "They do not have cloaks; but the wealthy are clad in silky garments that are short, tight-sleeved, and sewn up on all sides, so that they always move unimpeded."[15] A variety of fine silk clothing is available in more colors and designs than any other material. Favorites are scenes of African animals and birds, flowers and garden scenes, and one-of-a-kind designs such as Samson wrestling a lion or sailboats along the Bosphorus.

Carpets

Since you have come to Constantinople, Persian carpets must be on your shopping list. A sizable segment of the economy is based on the buying and selling of these beautiful works of art. In fact, one of the many jokes about the city is that if tourists accept directions from a stranger, they will find themselves in a carpet shop. There are so many shops that it is hard to return home without a carpet. Once shoppers enter, they are seated and given a cup of tea while carpets are lifted off piles by the owner's children and spread before the customers' feet.

Carpets, like silk fabrics, are one of the few commodities found in great supply in Constantinople that cannot be purchased elsewhere in Europe. Those looking for an astonishing addition to their homes will find the best selection of carpets at any of the large bazaars that line Mesê Street next to the Forum of Constantine in district number six. Like so much of the exotic merchandise found elsewhere in the city, carpets are handmade throughout Persia and India and then brought to Constantinople on the backs of camels that cross the deserts in long caravans.

Carpets from Persia and India are among the finest in the world, and they come in all sizes, types, quality, and colors. Potential buyers are advised to spend at least one entire day becoming familiar with them before entering into negotiations for one. The finest carpets are made from pure silk, wool, or combinations of the two. The two most desirable types are the knotted and the flat woven. For the knotted type, the knots used are normally the *sinneh,* in which the wool or silk thread forms a single turn about the warp thread (those cotton threads that form the foundation of the carpet), and the *ghiordes,* in which the wool or silk is taken twice around two adjacent warp threads.

The dyes used to color the carpets are of the greatest importance in completing the effect. All dyes are made from natural raw materials, either plant or animal, such as roots, flowers, barks, leaves, and parts of marine shellfish.

Beautiful carpets from Persia and India are available nowhere else in Europe.

The motifs that are found are usually unique to a particular village, and knowledgeable connoisseurs can identify the village where a carpet was made by its design. The most common and popular designs are those with flowers linked by tendrils, those depicting animals and people, and ones displaying geometric motifs. One popular design is a diamond motif using light or dark blue highlights on a background of red with added decorations of stylized plants and flowers. The borders often consist of a number of narrow bands framing a wider band, which is often decorated with motifs resembling pine or palm leaves. In some regions, more attention is paid to the pattern and in others to the coloring. Shoppers should note that the more distinct the pattern is on the underside of the work, the better the quality of the entire carpet.

Unlike most other goods that can be purchased in the city, large superb-quality carpets can take a single skilled weaver up to four years to complete. A skilled weaver is capable of tying eight thousand knots in a day, which for the finest and most dense carpets will represent only twelve square inches. The purchase of such a treasure that represents a significant part of the weaver's life will cost the buyer many *solidi,* and is something of a sacred act taken very seriously by any merchant in the city. Do not express an interest in purchasing a carpet unless your desire is genuine.

Illuminated Manuscripts

Scholars and other vacationers interested in purchasing a handwritten book, called a manuscript, have a variety of shops called *scriptoria* to choose from, or they can be purchased at the Studite Monastery where monks perform the copy work. Manuscripts are, with few exceptions, the most expensive purchases visitors can make. The cost depends upon the length of the book, the color of the ink, the quality of the vellum, and whether the work contains artistically painted color pictures called illuminations. Expect to pay dearly for fine-quality illuminated manuscripts. Scholar Arethas of Caesarea paid twenty *solidi* on average for his manuscripts, about a third of which went for the vellum. For this reason, few can afford large private collections such as that of

For those with discriminating taste, manuscripts can be ordered containing illustrations touched with gold and lapis lazuli.

Eustathios Boilas who boasts of owning one of the largest in Constantinople—eighty-one works.

The first step in this complicated process is to determine what book is wanted. The most often-requested manuscripts are copies of Homer's *Iliad*, Plato's *Dialogues,* and both the Old and New Testaments of the Bible. Next comes the the selection of the vellum, the goat and sheep skins that are soaked, scraped, dried, and treated before becoming the manuscript pages. Once selected, the pages will have margins on them, and the customer will determine the size and style of the lettering to be used. The stack of vella is then handed to scribes who perform the copying in black ink with quill pens, typically nine words to the line. When the scribes are finished, the pages are proofread, and any pages with errors are removed and replaced with corrected pages. The skins are then turned over to a team of illuminators. This is the step that will most affect the price of the manuscript.

The colors and degree of detail are determined by the customer according to his purse. Red, green, and blue are the most often-requested colors, but blue is the most expensive because the illuminator, who makes his own paints, grinds into the ink bits of the rare, blue stone, lapis lazuli, which costs double its weight in gold. For some especially elaborate books, customers may request highlights of gold leaf, which add a sparkle to the page.

The finished pages leave the illuminator's hands and are turned over to the

Covers decorated with diamonds and religious figures protect and complement illuminated manuscripts.

binder. Most often, illuminated manuscripts are bound between oak boards that are themselves decorated with brass and jewels. They often also have brass corner pieces to protect and hold together the boards. Finally, for an extra payment, the edges of the bound pages may be gilded to keep dust out of the book.

The Spice Market

Less expensive and easier to locate than manuscript makers are the spice merchants. Their fragrances act as a harbinger announcing their presence blocks before shoppers encounter them. Without question the most aromatic district in the city is number one, the same district encompassing the Imperial Palace. Spice merchants and perfume vendors are the only major markets allowed so close to the imperial residence because the pleasing aromas do not offend the royal family. In fact, the exotic scents are a symbol of luxury that befits the emperor and his court.

Spices are sought for use in medicine, perfume, embalming, dyes, and, of course, food seasonings. Each market stall sells a variety of spices, some of which are common to Constantinople and some that are quite rare. Regardless of their availability here, all are considered rare throughout Europe. Even pepper, which can be found in most homes in Constantinople, is rare

The Spice Route

Along with Alexandria, Egypt, Constantinople is a prominent gateway to Europe for the spice trade. All spices begin their journey from India, China, Burma, and a variety of islands throughout Indonesia. The spices make their way to Constantinople by first being transported by merchant freighters crossing the Bay of Bengal, then traversing the Arabian Sea, and then sailing up the Red Sea to the very end (just southwest of Cairo). Here all spice chests—made of heavy wood and sealed with pitch and tar to prevent moisture from entering—are loaded on camels and transported sixty miles northwest to Egypt's major port city of Alexandria (on the Mediterranean). There ships await the cargo bound for Constantinople.

The merchants who finance the shipping of spice chests stand to make a great deal of money—if the spices ever reach their destinations. Piracy takes a heavy toll on freighters in the Arabian and Red Seas, far from the protection of Constantinople's warships, which can only patrol the Aegean Sea and parts of the Mediterranean. Theft among the crews and even the captains causes shipowners and merchants to nervously await long-overdue ships and to sometimes abandon the possibility of ever seeing them arrive.

The spice chest, when well sealed, could float for long periods without damaging the contents. Knowing this, crew members sometimes manage to toss a few chests overboard at prearranged points close to the coast during the night. Accomplices on shore row small boats out into the water the next day in hopes of finding the chests and fishing them out of the water. One ten-pound chest of a spice could easily sell for an amount greater than a lifetime of wages for an average worker.

The cost and risk of spice shipping is high. Although insurance can be purchased and mercenaries hired to protect the shipments, even these measures cannot always prevent spice merchants from going bankrupt. No experienced merchant expects to see all of his spice chests arrive safely. Still, the profits are so high that even if six boats loaded with spices set sail for Constantinople and only one arrives, the merchant will still make a small profit.

and expensive in faraway, less cosmopolitan cities such as London, Paris, and Rome (where individual peppercorns are used as money for purchasing other commodities).

Spice merchants will do whatever is necessary to lure foreign travelers into their tents. In no other area is competition among merchants more aggressive. Be prepared to be pulled into their shops with a tug at your sleeve by a young child or by graceful women tempting you with a pinch of a sweet-smelling spice rubbed just under your nose. Moving straight ahead will help avoid being cajoled into one of the shops, but once you decide to enter a tent and make a purchase, the experience will be enjoyable and unforgettable.

The spice merchant will offer you a chair and ask you to be seated. Then a wood board, called a spice board, will be set out in front of you. The board has eight to ten small indentations, each filled with a small ground sample of one of the merchant's common but fragrant spices such as pepper, clove, ginger, nutmeg, cinnamon, or cardamom. Smell each sample until one, two, or perhaps three catch your attention. Then haggling for the best prices begins. Bargaining is always a good-spirited adventure, yet with so many shops to choose from, the tactic of standing up to leave will often force the merchant to lower the price. Once a price is agreed upon, the merchant will produce a small brass balance from beneath his bench, and the agreed upon amount of whole spice, not ground, is weighed. The reason only whole spice is sold is because it will remain fresh for many months until it is ground for use.

If the most exotic and most expensive spices are of interest, you must ask for them. The merchant keeps such spices hidden until specifically requested. Saffron, for example, that comes from the bright red stigmas of the saffron crocus plant, is artistically packaged to appear like miniature peacock fans and will cost more than many fine dinners—expect to pay as much as a *solidus* for a small amount. When a price and quantity are agreed upon, the merchant will again produce his brass balance to weigh each purchase. Rest assured that the balances are very accurate; the penalty for cheating a customer is quite severe—the loss of a hand or arm in most cases.

Clothes

The essential articles of clothing seen everywhere on the streets of Constantinople can be found throughout the city. The primary article of dress is the *tunica*, which serves as the basic undergarment of both men and women, or the only garment for the working class and poor. The main overgarment worn both by men and women of higher classes is called the *dalmatica*. The essential design of a *dalmatica* is triangular, with narrowing or flaring sleeves. An overgarment for women only is the *stola*, which is essentially unchanged from Roman times. Prior to the seventh century, the *stola* was the only overgarment for women. In the seventh and eighth centuries it developed bell-shaped sleeves and became undistinguishable from the *dalmatica*. Outer wear, which can be very ornate and expensive since it symbolizes personal wealth, consists of different style cloaks. The most popular of these is the *paludamentum* in semicircular or trapezoid shapes and the *paenula*, a full-circle cloak. The choice of fabrics will always determine the cost of clothing. The most expensive is silk, then wool, and finally Egyptian cotton.

Accessories are as popular as the main garments. Accessories are only for the

The selection of fabric, color, and embroidery distinguishes the clothing of class and wealth.

Constantinopolitans are very fond of vibrant, bright colors, reserving purple exclusively for the royal family. The association of purple with royalty is so strong and widely acknowledged that royal persons are often refered to by the color alone. Not long ago, in 968, the respected bishop of Cremona, Liutprand, visited Constantinople and commented on a wedding between a royal daughter and a foreigner, "It is an unheard of thing that a daughter born in the purple of an emperor born in the purple should be joined in marriage with strange nations."[16]

In addition to the color purple, the most exquisitely and richly ornamented clothing with gold embroidery and trimmed with jewels is also reserved for royalty. Beware of anyone who might try to sell you such ornate purple clothing. The selling of such "forbidden garments" to commoners is a crime. Violations are dealt with harshly; the law specifies, "Amputation of the offending hand which is dealt out to foreigners and to those who dyed cloth a forbidden color or made up forbidden garments."[17]

Shopping for exotic goods to take home may not be on everyone's agenda. If spending time and money being entertained seems more worthwhile, Constantinople has many forms from which to choose. Each is not intended to interest everyone, but everyone will be able to find several that will be enjoyable and memorable.

wealthy, and they include the *sudarium*, an elaborate embroidered handkerchief; the *contabulatim*, a long, embroidered cloth that is fan-folded and wound around the body; the *pallium*, a very rich, long, jeweled outer garment, like a vest, worn by men; and the *superhumeral*, an elaborate embroidered and sometimes jeweled collar.

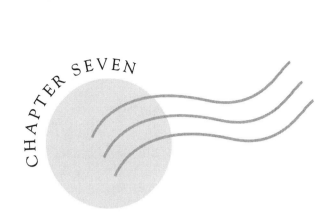

CHAPTER SEVEN

Entertainment

Entertainment of many types can be found in Constantinople. Not all, however, are available to tourists who are here for a few days or a week. Hunting, for example, that requires a horse, knowledge of the local terrain, and weaponry normally not carried by vacationers, would not be a good choice for average tourists. However, there are many less demanding diversions that ought to satisfy everyone's idea of fun.

A Day at the Chariot Races

Chariot races are the favorite sport of Constantinopolitans. Races are held at the Hippodrome about 110 days a year, ensuring most visitors at least one opportunity to enjoy this colorful, spectacular event. Be aware that races are primarily attended by men. Women who sit in the crowd should expect to experience leering and catcalls from male patrons because most women who attend the races are considered to be of low moral character. Still, the races are

a rewarding outing. Plan to spend the entire day, and bring some money for a midday snack at one of dozens of food stalls circling the stadium—and a little extra for wagering.

Each race features twelve chariots, either two-horse or four-horse chariots. The chariots are little more than two wheels joined by an axle that is attached to the halters of the horses by a wooden bar. The charioteer stands on a small wooden platform, no larger than his two feet, with nothing to steady him. This flimsy construction, intended to reduce weight and increase speed, offers the charioteer nothing to hold onto other than the reins that control the horses; balance is crucial for winning and survival. First-time spectators can expect to see at least a few charioteers carried from the Hippodrome injured or even worse.

The start of a race is signaled by the entry of the horses and chariots to the starting box at the northeastern end,

Liabilities of the Sport of Hunting

Sometimes sporting events turn sour. Even emperors live with the possibility, although remote, that they might be injured or killed while enjoying one of their favorite pastimes, such as hunting. In 886, Emperor Basil I, the emperor who began the Golden Age of Constantinople, was gored and killed while partaking in his favorite sport, deer hunting. The tragic event was recorded by Euthymius I, patriarch of Constantinople:

It was August and the Emperor Basil had gone out for the hunt, into Thrace, to the neighborhood of Melitias. Finding a herd of deer, but he gave chase with the Senate and the huntsman. They were all scattered in every direction in pursuit, when the emperor spurred after the leader of the herd, whose size and sleekness made him conspicuous. He was giving chase alone, for his companions were tired; but the stag, seeing him isolated, turned in his flight, and charged, trying to gore him; he threw his spear, but the stag's antlers were in the way, and it glanced off useless to the ground. The emperor now, finding himself helpless, took to flight; but the deer, pursuing, struck at him with its antlers and carried him off. For the tips of the antlers having slipped under his belt, the stag lifted him from his horse and bore him away, and no one knew this had happened, until they saw the horse riderless. Then, one of the Farghanese [a huntsman with the emperor], managed to ride up alongside the deer and with a naked hand, cut the horn-entangled belt through. The emperor fell to the ground unconscious.

A stag attacks a member of royalty during a hunt. Hunting is a sport that is fraught with danger.

where they are lined up behind a taut rope. While the horses line up, the crowd wildly begins to place bets on their favorite teams. When all is ready, watch for the starter to drop the *mappa,* a white scarf. The moment the scarf hits the ground, the rope is dropped and the chariots thunder down the track kicking up the yellow sand and cedar chips of the track as they round the far turn and come back down the straightaway. Successfully negotiating each tight turn is where races are won or lost and where charging horses are most likely to collide, flipping over their chariots and drivers. There are eight races each day, and the number of laps for each race varies from two to six.

For those new to the city who choose to attend the races, be advised that spectators take their favorite teams seriously. More than merely chariot teams, the Red, White, Blue, and Green teams are also political factions and from time to time supporters engage in fistfights in the stands over the races or political opinions. Be aware of where you are sitting, and be smart about wagering on the same team as those sitting around you.

Jousting

The second favorite sporting activity that takes place in the Hippodrome and at the sports field at the Imperial Palace is jousting. This sport, although completely different from chariot racing, is no less dramatic and colorful. Like so many sports involving men and horses, jousting is a

The Emperor, high above the melee, watches a chariot race.

mandatory sport in the upbringing of a young aristocrat.

The object of the joust is for two mounted soldiers in full armor to charge each other with long lances. Each attempts to knock the other off his horse. In warfare, the lances have sharp iron tips capable of piercing armor and killing the opponent. Here at the Hippodrome, however, lances have blunt wood tips, and the winner is declared when one opponent is knocked from his horse. Nonetheless, a direct hit at full gallop will still injure an opponent but not mortally impale him.

One traveler to visit our city, Benjamin of Tudela, who watched the jousts on the field at the Imperial Palace, commented: "At Constantinople is the palace

Gala Entries

The drama of the arrival of a visiting dignitary is the best show the city has to offer. A spectacle such as this one is unforgettable entertainment well worth seeing if visitors are fortunate enough to be in the city at the time. Foreign dignitaries receive the pomp and ceremony befitting their office; the higher their status, the larger the entourage that rides out to escort them into the city and the more elaborate the reception when they arrive.

These celebrations are well-planned gala events gauged to impress the visiting dignitaries as well as to entertain Constantinopolitans. On the day of arrival, banners announcing the celebrated event, made of silk and woven wool, are flung down from windows and balconies of houses and shops along the parade route. The ceremony begins when the dignitary is within a day's ride of the city. The emperor then dispatches a regiment of the Imperial Guard to escort the distinguished guest through the Golden Gate, the most magnificent and most celebrated of all the city's gates. Citizens gather at the gate and all along the parade route, Mesê Street, to catch a glimpse of the entourage.

The entourage passes through the Golden Gate escorted by the Imperial Guard carrying gold-tipped lances and wearing full-dress uniforms featuring gold helmets with crests and gold breastplates worn over white tunics. Their horses, equally resplendent, are regally caparisoned with saddles, blankets, and halters bearing the crest of the emperor. As this impressive regal escort departs the Golden Gate and begins to move down Mesê Street, a riderless white horse, selected from the emperor's stable, is brought to the honored guest for the short ride to the Imperial Palace.

Spectators lining the street jostle each other to catch a glimpse of the dignitary and to cheer the procession, while people on balconies throw white bits of silk that drift down like snowflakes upon the horses and riders. When the procession reaches the Imperial Palace, it is met by the emperor. He wears his most ornate ceremonial robes, strewn with jewels, which prompted one anonymous visitor to describe it as "A meadow covered in flowers."

of the emperor, right fair and well-dight [designed]: and therein is a fair place for joustings, or for other plays and desports [sports]. And under these stages be stables well vaulted for the emperor's horses; and all the pillars be of marble."[18]

Leading participants, usually nobility, enjoy the fame that the jousts bring to gallant competitors. Champions, who become famous and wealthy from winning many jousts, sometimes also become arrogant about their successes and riches. The eleventh-century historian Niketas Choniates noticed this trend when he described one young nobleman as entering the Hippodrome, "Grinning a little as usual and grasping his pike [lance] . . . wearing a fashionable cloak pinned at the right shoulder . . . and his fair-maned horse was adorned with gold trappings that vied with his noble rider's array."[19] But as Choniates continued his description of the gallant, grinning, well-dressed combatant, things did not go well when he "was thrown from his saddle like a ball, tumbling on his neck and shoulders. Pale with fear he tried to cover himself with his shield."[20]

Polo Contests

For visitors interested in equine sporting events, but not keen on the roughness of the chariot races and jousts, watching a game of polo may provide a more civilized diversion. Polo matches are played at one of two large venues: the polo field within the Imperial Palace and the field just outside the Gate of Charisius, at the end of Mesê Street. Although polo has been popular in Constantinople since the reign of Emperor Justinian, few play the game because of the cost of the horses and because of the large field needed, roughly 300 by 150 yards. A visitor's best bet is to inquire at the Chalkê Gate for the time of the next match. The field can be found just north of the lighthouse next to the water.

The object of the game, which originated in Asia many centuries ago, is for one team of four horsemen to hit a small ball with a wood stick through the opponent's goal. The rules are simple for this game that began as a way for cavalry soldiers to train for battle in times of peace. The first ball used in Constantinople was called a pala ($\pi\acute{\alpha}\lambda\alpha$), named for the pala tree that grows in the surrounding countryside from which the ball and sticks are made. Gradually, the game became known as pala; now we know it as polo.

Visitors watching a match at the Imperial Palace will enjoy a display of horsemanship by the princes within the royal family as well as a display of the family's finest horses, some of which fetch as much as one thousand *solidi* when sold. Such an expense explains the game's unofficial name: the Sport of Kings. On this field the royal family and guests sit in a single enclosed portico the length of the field. The goalposts at either end are made of marble.

The excitement of the game is watching these one-thousand-pound horses running up and down the field at full

Princes of Constantinople's royal family engage in a polo match. Polo is a centuries-old game known today as the Sport of Kings.

speed, often colliding with one another and sometimes spilling riders onto the grass. As the riders strike the ball to teammates, eventually someone hits the ball through the two posts for a score. Every seven minutes the teams stop to mount fresh horses. Following six periods of play, everyone gathers for refreshments.

Public Punishment

For any visitors who find all of the equine sports much too tame, a day watching a variety of public punishments might be more invigorating. While wandering the streets, if you happen to see soldiers leading a donkey carrying two men bound back to back, you are witnessing two

criminals being escorted to their public punishment. Join the crowd that always follows them if you wish.

Violators of some of the lesser laws in Constantinople can expect to be punished in a variety of ways, but violators of more serious laws can expect to die for their crimes. Public punishment for lesser crimes takes place at the Amastrian Forum located on Mesê Street and occasionally on the street itself.

The punishments that take place along Mesê Street are typically some type of public humiliation or infliction of pain. Most commonly seen during the day is the humiliation of men forced to dress as women and made to parade through the streets to the jeers and delight of the crowds. Sometimes the men's heads are shaved as a way of temporarily branding them as outlaws, a humiliation that lasts for several weeks until their hair grows back. Men suffering this indignation frequently exile themselves rather than suffer the daily taunts and barbs of neighbors and strangers alike. For more serious offenses, pain and permanent bodily disfigurement are inflicted. Often seen are amputations of a limb—either a hand, arm, or foot by sword—or the gouging of one or both eyes.

By everyone's standards, however, the most macabre and popular form of public punishment is the execution. Punishment of serious crimes that prescribe the death penalty are held in the Hippodrome as entertainment between chariot races. Although such executions are intended to deter others who might be tempted to commit the same crime, nonetheless crowds flock to the Hippodrome to enjoy them. The luckier victims are simply beheaded; this is the fastest and least painful of all techniques. Death by impalement is worse because it is not as quick. The victim, made to sit on the sharpened tip of a long pike that slowly penetrates his body as far as his chest cavity, slowly dies from internal bleeding. The worst fate is to be thrown to a variety of ferocious animals that fight over and tear at the victim. The crowds, entirely lacking any compassion, cheer and sometimes burst into laughter as the condemned man is dismembered while still alive.

A Day at the Baths

For those seeking civility, few activities in Constantinople will provide a more pleasant and satisfying indulgence after a long day venturing through the city's shopping districts than a few hours at one of the many public or private baths. Visitors who have friends or family belonging to one of the more than one hundred private baths may enjoy a small, more intimate bathing experience. Do not be surprised to see elegant women dressed in silk brocade on their way to one of the elite private baths, such as the Baths of Zeuxippus, while reclining in a donkey-drawn carriage. For visitors who cannot gain entry into one of the posh private baths, several large public baths can be just as enjoyable at a fraction of the cost.

Attending a bathing complex is like enjoying an afternoon at a club. These structures, some of which are large enough to accommodate several thousand bathers at a time, provide an environment that includes bathing pools, massage salons, restaurants, a library and reading room, a wrestling pit, and conference rooms where business negotiations often take place.

Typically men and women enter separate bathing complexes and immediately proceed to a room called the *apodyterium* where they remove their clothes and place them in a locker. From there they enter the first of three pools called the *calidarium*. The hot water in the *calidarium* is heated by channels under the floor through which hot air circulates to heat

In a public bath a visitor can bathe, get a massage, read a manuscript from the library, eat a meal, or watch a wrestling match.

the marble floor of the pool. After ten or fifteen minutes, bathers move to a pool filled with tepid water called the *tepidarium* and then to the room with the frigid water pool called the *frigidarium* for a short but refreshing plunge. The last step in this routine is a rubdown with olive oil that removes dirt and grime from the pores of the skin. The oil and dirt are then removed with a strigil, a curved scraper made of wood, and the bather returns to

the *apodyterium* to dress and move on to one of many more activities.

Most bathers spend from two to four hours at a bath, but some visitors find enough activities to occupy the entire day. Since the public baths are paid for by tax money, the cost of entry for the day is only three *folleis*; that leaves money to spend on a massage, cool drink, or a meal.

The public baths are very much a microcosm of the city, and for this reason, a day at the baths may be the most fitting way to end a vacation in Constantinople. Much like the city itself, the baths have an international flavor where all nationalities can meet, enjoy exotic spiced foods, relax, and watch the colorful flow of people going about their lives. Constantinople has now flourished as an international destination for seven hundred years and is suitably established, positioned, and valued to retain its title of Queen of Cities for a very long time.

Notes

Introduction: The Queen of Cities

1. Quoted in Dean A. Miller, *Imperial Constantinople*. New York: Wiley & Sons, 1969, p. 6.

Chapter One: A Brief History of Constantinople

2. Quoted in Paul Halsall, "Sozomen (d.c. 450 CE): Constantine Founds Constantinople, 324 CE," *Ancient History Source Book*, 1998. www.fordham.edu.

Chapter Two: Weather and Location

3. Quoted in Marcus Nathan Adler, *The Itinerary of Benjamin of Tudela: Critical Text, Translation and Commentary*. New York: Phillip Feldheim, 1907, p. 20.

4. Quoted in Philip Sherrard, *Byzantium*. New York: Time-Life Books, 1966, p. 33.

5. Quoted in A.P. Kazhdan and Ann Wharton Epstein, *Change in Byzantine Culture in the Eleventh and Twelfth Centuries*. Berkeley: University of California Press, 1985, p. 49.

6. Quoted in "Traveling to Jerusalem: Daniel of Russia," University of Southern Colorado Department of History. www.uscolo.edu.

Chapter Three: Arriving and Becoming Familiar with the City

7. Quoted in Miller, *Imperial Constantinople*, p. 139.

8. "Coins of the Byzantine Empire," *History & Numismatics*, 2002. www.wegm.com.

9. Kazhdan and Epstein, *Change in Byzantine Culture*, p. 104.

10. Quoted in Ernest F. Henderson, *Select Historical Documents of the Middle Ages*. London: George Bell, 1910, p. 452.

11. Quoted in J.M. Hussey, *The Byzantine World*. London: Hutchinson University Library, 1967, p. 126.

Chapter Four: Architectural Treasures

12. Quoted in Paul Halsath, "Procopios: on the Great Church," trans. W. Lethaby and H. Swainson. *Ancient History Source Book*, 1996. www.fordham.edu.

13. Quoted in Adler, *The Itinerary of Benjamin of Tudela*, p. 21.

Chapter Six: Shopping

14. Quoted in Adler, *The Itinerary of Benjamin of Tudela*, p. 23.

15. Quoted in Kazhdan and Epstein, *Change in Byzantine Culture*, p. 76.
16. Quoted in Henderson, *Select Historical Documents of the Middle Ages*, p. 449.
17. Quoted in Miller, *Imperial Constantinople*, p. 65.

Chapter Seven: Entertainment
18. Quoted in Adler, *The Itinerary of Benjamin of Tudela*, pp. 23–24.
19. Quoted in Kazhdan and Epstein, *Change in Byzantine Culture*, p. 109.
20. Quoted in Kazhdan and Epstein, *Change in Byzantine Culture*, p. 109.

For Further Reading

Book of the Prefect. Trans. A.E.R. Boak. Oxford: Oxford University Press, 1937. This sixth-century book provides a wealth of detailed information on commercial activity in Constantinople. It provides details on guilds, costs for materials, taxes, laws governing commerce, and many unusual provisions that shed light on the city's economics.

Guglielmo Cavallo, *The Byzantines*. Trans. Thomas Dunlap, Teresa Lavender Fagan, Charles Lambert. Chicago: University of Chicago Press, 1997. This book is a collection of studies highlighting nearly all aspects of ordinary Byzantine life. Cavallo gives the reader insights into paupers, peasants, soldiers, teachers, bureaucrats, clerics, and emperors. All of these segments of society, including both men and women, are given full and vivid descriptions.

George Ostrogorsky, *History of the Byzantine State*. Trans. Joan Hussey. New Brunswick, NJ: Rutgers University Press, 1969. Ostrogorsky's book has been a classic since its release. The large book covers all of Byzantine history from Diocletian and Constantine to the fall of Constantinople in 1453. It has always been considered one of the most intelligible and useful historical works for anyone interested in Byzantine history.

Steven Runciman, *Byzantine Civilization*. London: Edward Arnold Ltd., 1959. A great book that manages to provide a general picture of the civilization of the Eastern Roman Empire during the period when Constantinople was its capital. Runciman presents a balanced world covering the usual political and economic facets of the city but also literature, religion, and art of the period.

Works Consulted

Books

Marcus Nathan Adler, *The Itinerary of Benjamin of Tudela: Critical Text, Translation and Commentary.* New York: Phillip Feldheim, 1907. This book is an account of the eleventh-century traveler, Benjamin of Tudela, who traveled through the Mediterranean basin visiting all of the major cities and recoding his impressions. The value of the work rests with his observations of lifestyles and city monuments.

Ernest F. Henderson, *Select Historical Documents of the Middle Ages.* London: George Bell, 1910. Henderson's book is a selection of medieval historical documents that he has translated. Most of the documents are European, but the book contains a few describing Constantinople and the history surrounding the city and empire.

J.M. Hussey, *The Byzantine World.* London: Hutchinson University Library, 1967. The author provides an account of Byzantine culture from the foundation of the Empire in 330 to its downfall in 1453. The book provides excellent insight into various aspects of Byzantine political, religious, and cultural life.

A.P. Kazhdan and Ann Wharton Epstein, *Change in Byzantine Culture in the Eleventh and Twelfth Centuries.* Berkeley: University of California Press, 1985. This is an excellent book full of interesting ideas and interpretations of the history of eleventh- and twelfth-century Constantinople. The authors explore the period in great detail, discussing the social, economic, and intellectual history of the city and empire.

John Mandeville, *The Travels of Sir John Mandeville.* New York: Penguin Classics, 1984. Sir John Mandeville was an early-Renaissance English travel writer. His historical accuracy has been questioned by most historians, but his writings, nonetheless, present a live view of the Mediterranean and how people lived and traveled before the

Crusades. A copy of Mandeville's book was known to belong to Leonardo da Vinci.

Dean A. Miller, *Imperial Constantinople*. New York: Wiley & Sons, 1969. Miller provides an excellent scholarly history of the ancient city of Constantinople. Of particular interest are his detailed discussions of the economy, architecture, imperial families, and the bureaucratic organization of the empire.

Procopius, *De Aedificiis: The Church of St. Sophia Constantinople*. Trans. W. Lethaby and H. Swainson. New York: n.p., 1894. This book is one of the classic primary sources discussing the buildings in sixth-century Constantinople. Procopius walked through all of the buildings he describes and was one of the few historians of the time whose accounts have survived.

Tamar Talbot Rice, *Everyday Life in Byzantium*. London: B.T. Batsford Ltd., 1967. Rice provides an excellent description of the characteristics of both government and society of Constantinople during the tenth through twelfth centuries. The book has a unique focus on the political and cultural life of the city and empire that were modeled along Greek lines yet influenced by other peoples in the eastern Mediterranean.

Philip Sherrard, *Byzantium*. New York: Time-Life Books, 1966. Sherrard's book is one of the few works dealing with Constantinople and the Byzantine Empire that includes an adequate collection of maps and pictures to enhance the text. This is one of the better books available for young readers.

Strabo, *Strabo Geography*. Trans. Horace Jones. London: Loeb Classical Library, 1927. Strabo's work is one of the few early discussions about the geography of the eastern Mediterranean that also gives a brief history of each region that he describes, as well as occasional discussions of the flora and fauna.

Websites

Ancient History Source Book (www.fordham.edu). This site is associated with Fordham University and provides a broad selection of primary sources translated into English. It covers most major areas of ancient history with emphasis on ancient Europe and the Middle East.

History & Numismatics (www.wegm.com). This website provides a brief history of several eastern Mediterranean civilizations along with a small example of coinage, which includes close-up color photographs.

University of Southern Colorado Department of History (www.uscolo.edu). This website provides links to many of the history department's programs and to the many history projects ongoing at the university.

Index

Picture Credits

About the Author

James Barter received his undergraduate degree in history and classics at the University of California (Berkeley) followed by graduate studies in ancient history and archaeology at the University of Pennsylvania. Mr. Barter has taught history as well as Latin and Greek.

A Fulbright scholar at the American Academy in Rome, Mr. Barter worked on archaeological sites in and around the city as well as on sites in the Naples area. Mr. Barter also has worked and traveled extensively in Greece.

Mr. Barter currently lives in Rancho Santa Fe, California, with his seventeen-year-old daughter Kalista who is a student at Torrey Pines High School and works as a soccer referee while considering her college options. Mr. Barter's older daughter, Tiffany Deal, lives nearby with her husband, Mike, and she teaches classical violin and sells meteorites.